A WAGGONER'S WAR

1st Edition
published in 2011 by

Woodfield Publishing Ltd
Bognor Regis PO21 5EL England
www.woodfieldpublishing.co.uk

ISBN 1-84683-116-4

Printed and bound in England

Cover design by Mike Rowland

A Waggoner's War

A Motor Transport Driver's Experiences in North Africa and Italy with the Royal Army Service Corps –1942-45

FERGUS FULTON

Woodfield

Woodfield Publishing Ltd

Bognor Regis ~ West Sussex ~ England ~ PO21 5EL
tel 01243 821234 ~ e/m info@woodfieldpublishing.co.uk

Interesting and informative books on a variety of subjects

For full details of all our published titles, visit our website at
www.woodfieldpublishing.co.uk

To the memory of Fergus and Jessie Fulton

"Bombing was not new to me, but the whine of Jerry's 88s sent shivers up and down my spine. Before the Tunisian campaign had finished I too had learned to live under fire as if nothing unusual was going on, but there were many times when one felt that peculiar feeling in the stomach, even towards the end of the war."

~ CONTENTS ~

Fergus with his eldest son Gordon, London 1958.

Preface

Fergus Fulton, the author of this book, died in 1976. I knew he had kept a diary of his wartime experiences but I'd never got round to actually reading it. I was young and had young things to do, although I had always been fascinated by the German binoculars, the German army belt with *Gott Mit Uns* on it, the telegraph headphones that lay out in the garage and the ship in a bottle made by a prisoner of war, which was probably exchanged for cigarettes and chocolate. Eventually, in the 1980s, I developed a love of history and realised I possessed something unique that I had always taken for granted on my own doorstep, or, more accurately, tucked away on a shelf in a cupboard. I read it and loved it. My dad's neat handwriting and unfussy style really brought the vivid images to life. I then put it away again. Twenty years on, with the acquisition of a computer, I had the idea to type it up and find a publisher for it, which I did. I felt it was a story worth sharing with a larger readership, be they part of the dwindling band of veterans, or simply younger people with a curiosity about the brave men who fought in the Second World War and helped to keep our country free of tyranny. It was a pleasure and honour to put it together.

I've kept the spelling of place names and the punctuation and grammar exactly as they were in the original diaries for the sake of authenticity. My only regret is not having my dad here to ask him more details, to fill in some of the gaps, particularly about his stay in Austria prior to demobilisation which is only briefly mentioned. What was being in a war like? How scared were you? What do you remember the most? I'd also like to think I could have carried out my job under those circumstances as well as he did, but I doubt it. It never ceases to astonish me how these men just seemed to take it all in their stride and then go back to their 'normal' lives when they got home. I should have asked him about it all when he was here. However, it's back in the past and I'm just thankful to have this volume containing these lines which at least tell some of the story of one man's 'ordinary' war.

Graham Fulton

About the Author

Fergus Fulton was born in Valparaiso, Chile, in 1923, the only child of Daniel and Maud Fulton. They eventually moved to Scotland, where Daniel had originally come from, in 1931. They settled in Glasgow where Fergus completed his education and also developed a love for cycling, the countryside, music, drawing and writing stories. He got a job with J and P Coats, the thread manufacturers, in 1940. In 1942, aged 19, he joined the R.A.S.C. and served throughout the North African and Italian campaigns.

After demobilisation he returned to work with J and P Coats in Paisley, and it was here he met and fell in love with Jessie McLardie. They were married on June 25th 1948 at the High Church in Paisley. Over the years his job took him to London where they lived in the 1950s and where their two boys Gordon and Graham were born in 1957 and 1959 respectively. They moved back north to Paisley in 1962. He continued working for J and P Coats and became one of their most loyal, respected and hard-working salesmen.

He also continued with his love of music and literature and was an active member of the Masons. He always wanted to travel abroad again but the other great adventure of his life, bringing up and looking after a young family, took up his time and he never did. Fergus died of a heart attack during the summer of 1976, aged 53. His wife Jessie outlived him by 27 years and in the 1990s made an emotional visit to Rome and Florence to see the places he had told her about and had always wanted to show her.

Fergus and Jessie on their wedding day, 25th June 1948.

1.   NORTH AFRICA

IN TRANSIT

RHKOH Draft, consisting of approximately 150 all ranks, marched off from Ronsoy House, Woking, to the mess room in the town for supper, and then proceeded to the goods station to entrain. There was no singing on the march, and in the station we talked quietly, moved little, and could not smoke. It was supposed to be a "secret" move, although it was of course a well-known fact in the town that an overseas draft was moving out. Eventually, about 9 p.m. on November 25th 1942, we entrained and commenced our long, eventful Odyssey. In the early morning we reached Newcastle, then on to Waverley Station, Edinburgh. From there we crossed over to Wishaw, where we de-trained and straggled up to the Transit Camp at the old brewery. That night most men whose homes were in the Glasgow area took the chance of going home for a couple of hours.

On the morning of the 27th we entrained again along with some infantry reinforcement drafts, and travelled on through Glasgow and Paisley to Gourock.

Here we boarded the river boat "Antelope" and sailed round the anchorage calling at several of the ships in the convoy until we heaved to alongside the Union-Castle liner "Llangibby Castle", and embarked on our new home. We lay all day in the bay watching the submarines and Catalina flying-boats, and speculating on our destination, which we had decided wasn't going to be Northern Ireland after all.

Our living quarters were a mess deck in the bowels of the ship, where we slept, had our meals, spent our evenings, and did our fatigues. At night it was a mass of swinging hammocks, sweltering heat, and rotten atmosphere. This existed all the time we were on the ship, which we re-named the "Altmark", and not without reason.

Apart from these uncomfortable (to say the least of it!) living quarters, we had very short rations and badly cooked meals, no canteen, and bad sanitary arrangements.

The latrines were filthy, and the washrooms were not nearly sufficient for the number of men. If you got up at 6 o'clock and stood in the washroom queue you stood a reasonable chance of getting a wash before 8 o'clock, but at the risk of losing your breakfast. There were nearly 3,000 men on board, with life-boats to accommodate 700, which made us wrinkle our brows a bit. However, there were quite a number of rafts.

When we awoke on the morning of the 28th we found we were at sea and out of sight of land. There were about 30 ships in the convoy, with several destroyers and corvettes escorting us far out on the horizon. For the first three or four days the weather kept pretty good, but as we were skirting the Bay of Biscay a regular gale came up, and for two days we took a considerable amount of battering. On the first night of the storm I was on guard, which turned out to be about the worst guard I've ever done. The guard-room was below the foc'sle in the bows of the ship, and we had our work cut out to prevent ourselves from rolling across the floor every time the ship heaved.

On the night of Friday December 4th, the two most memorable incidents of the voyage occurred. We were approaching the

Straits of Gibraltar, and on the starboard side we could see the lights on the coast of Spanish Morocco, and on the port side the dark coast of Spain. The finest sight of all was the free city of Tangier, with its twinkling lights mounting up till they mingled with the stars. Not only was it our first sight of land, but it brought back memories of peacetime and made us realise what a gloomy thing is the black-out.

The time would be about 10 p.m. when we had just passed through the straits, and all the lads were below decks once again, most of them getting ready for bed or already in their hammocks. I was sitting reading and thinking about turning in, when all of a sudden we felt a dull thud which caused the ship to shudder, then a crash and she listed sharply to starboard. The lights all went off for about thirty seconds, then fortunately came on again. My first impression, like most of the other fellows, was that either we had been torpedoed or struck a mine. My feelings in the first instant were of disappointment rather than of fear; having seen the shores of Africa earlier in the evening had made me feel that we had come through the voyage without any trouble, and now, on the last lap, we were to be beaten. I grabbed my life-jacket and joined the line of blokes who were rushing upstairs. When I reached the well-deck and looked round I saw the shape of another ship slowly drawing away from us, and I realised that we had been involved in a collision. A few minutes later we were told over the loudspeaker that there was no immediate danger and were instructed to return to our mess decks. The bulkheads had been closed, but in 7 minutes the water in the hold had risen to a level of 18 ft. We were not long below decks before the loudspeaker told us to "Report to boat stations, prepare to abandon ship." Without any panic or excitement we filed up the companion-way and stood at our raft positions.

A Lance Corporal called the roll, the only man missing being our section officer, Captain Michael Beer, whom I had the misfortune to meet again two years later. We stood by our raft for about half an hour while the ship signalled to the rest of the convoy, then the ship's C.O. Lt/Col. Ritchie, came round and told us that the danger was over and we could go back to bed. The ship was going to put into Gibraltar for repairs. I climbed into my hammock but left my clothes on, and was soon asleep.

Next morning we were lying in the outer bay of Gibraltar, and gradually we moved into the harbour inside the mole. It was a dull and wet day, but the Rock was a fine sight, and it was interesting to watch the movements of the many battleships, submarines, flying-boats and foreign merchant ships. Soldiers on the docks, however, told us it was a rotten place to be stationed in. We lay here for a day. Apparently, to pass through the Straits our convoy had moved into single file, and having passed through our ship was speeding up to resume its former position in the convoy when it crossed the path of a Polish merchant ship, and the collision resulted. The starboard bow of the ship was badly damaged, and if we had been in the heavy swell of the Atlantic when the collision took place, we would certainly have foundered. The crew's quarters in the foc'sle were in a bit of a mess, and the off-duty watch were lucky to have been sitting round a table in the middle of the floor playing cards when the collision occurred, as all their bunks had been sandwiched together, and anyone lying in bed would have been crushed to death.

That night we were all transported from the "Llangibby Castle" to her sister ship the "Llanstephan Castle", which was now so overcrowded that our living quarters had to be the Officers' lounge, where we slept on sofas and had the use of tables and chairs etc, which was to us comparative luxury. On the evening of December 6th we sailed in company of one other ship and two corvettes to make the journey across the Mediterranean to Africa. On the morning of December 8th we arrived at Algiers.

We lay out in the bay for some time until an assault craft, or "invasion barge" as they were then called, came out from the docks and pulled alongside of us. The R.A.S.C. were the first to disembark, and it was a ticklish job to walk down the gangway and jump from there on to the side of the ship in the swell. About 100 of us got into the barge and made the trip to the docks, and it was a grand feeling to be on "terra firma" again. On the mole we found a party of sailors who had been there since the first day of the invasion and were doing guards in the docks. Our first contact with the Algerian population was when a number of dirty Arab kids crowded round the gate of the mole offering oranges for sale. In the meantime, our barge had returned to the ship to take off the rest of our draft, but after about an hour it returned empty. One of the usual blunders had taken place, and the ship had gone off to Bone, further down the Algerian coast, taking the rest of the draft with it. We spent about two hours on the docks while our officer was finding out what the next move was to be, and finally it was ascertained that our camp was at a village named La Perouse, about 15 miles further along the coast. As it was pouring rain, we were glad when our officer decided to make the trip by barge instead of marching, so we piled into our craft once more and set off across the bay. It was a terrible trip, and one or two fellows were horribly sick over the side, but finally we arrived at our destination and disembarked. It may be as well to note that we had arrived in North Africa to join the 1st Army and take part in one of the most gruelling campaigns of the war, but our scale of equipment suggested rather that we were all going on leave. We had rifles, but no bayonets and not a round of ammunition between us. We were to live in the open, but not one of us had a groundsheet to lie on. As soon as we had all landed in La Perouse, we were issued with bivouac tents (about 6 ft. x 4ft.), one between three men, but no poles to erect them with. So we hunted for some bamboo canes, and eventually managed to throw the tent up. Our camp was on a rain-soaked, muddy hillside, we had two damp blankets each, and our clothes and kit were already soaked through, so we were quite resigned to having a rotten night. That evening we had our first meal of dog biscuits and bully beef, which we were to become quite familiar with in the succeeding months. We laid our gas capes down in lieu of groundsheets, which was rather useless as there were several little rivulets running through the middle of our tent. During the night one of our neighbours who had been sampling some of the French wine in the café on the beach was staggering round the camp looking for his "bivvy" when he fell over ours and brought the whole thing down on top of us, so we had to turn out in the darkness and rain and go through the process of erecting it again! When I thought later on of our first night in North Africa, I was amazed that we did not feel as depressed as we could have done.

The following morning we moved into a disused shed on·the beach, which was a considerable improvement on the bivouacs.

We had discovered by now that we were in No.1 General Base Depot and were to wait here until we were posted to working units. We lived in this hut on the beach for two days while I.P. Tents (or "cottage" tents) were being erected. On our third day here a parade was held, at which the camp Colonel (an R.A.C. man) decided that in case of a counter-invasion on the coast by the Germans the R.A.S.C. were to be the first line of defence so we were the only ones with rifles, and the Royal Armoured Corps were to be the second line as they had revolvers. So after that it was decided to issue us with 10 rounds of ammo apiece, and give us daily spells of rifle and foot drill, route marches, and general items of "bull." The only saving grace about life in the camp was the well-stocked Café, where we had our first taste of the excellent Muscatel wine. We went swimming in the daytime in the Mediterranean, and at the lunch-hour had Orangeade or Muscatel with frog sandwiches at the "Hotel de la Plage".

On December 14th all the R.A.S.C. personnel were disposed of by being sent on detachment. I went with about 40 others to 931 General Transport Coy. in Algiers. We were taken in civilian buses to their H.Q. in the Zoological Gardens, where we were sorted out and posted to the various platoons. I went to "C" Platoon with about 9 others, and was billeted in the club house of the Racquette Tennis Club, situated at La Redoute, a suburb on the summit of the hill where the residential parts of Algiers are built. It was a comfortable billet compared to the camp of the past week, and we enjoyed watching the well-to-do French people playing tennis. We were all given a driving test and then allocated as second drivers to 6-ton diesels, Karriers, Dennisses, and Albions, on dock transport, carrying bombs, petrol, and rations from the docks to various dumps around Algiers. It was an experience driving 6 tonners on the right-hand side of unfamiliar roads and in the congested traffic of the Algiers streets.

We had several opportunities of taking a few hours off, which we spent roaming around the town. Of course, it was less than a month since the invasion and entertainment for the troops was not yet organised, but there was plenty to see in the town. We visited 'Monoprix', the French Woolworth's, and 'La Poste', the G.P.O. from the roof of which Vichy snipers operated against our assault troops. We also went round the Musée, the Arab graveyard, the University, and the Government houses where Darlan was later on assassinated. The main streets are not very wide but are very pleasant with trees all along the pavements, a thing never seen in Britain.

Rue d'Isly is the most popular, and most of the cinemas are there. Luxurious cafés such as the "Black Cat" and "The Sphinx" are places which will never be forgotten by troops who were privileged to visit Algiers. One of our most interesting after-noons was when we unwittingly wandered into one of the streets of the Kasbah, the Arab quarter which was out-of-bounds to troops. The street was very narrow and absolutely filthy, rising all the time in gradual steps. It is said that "there are a thousand ways into the Kasbah and only one way out", but it is not strictly true, unless you are a fugitive from French justice. Dirty kids followed us, laughing and throwing snatches of English, asking if we wanted a shoe-shine or pointing out the brothels which seemed to be every other house in the street. Men and women eyed us without saying anything. We were unmolested, but the Americans were not liked, as some of them had tried to remove the veils which Arab women wear over their faces, and a number of stabbings had taken place.

Incidentally, the so-called "Arabs" of North Africa are not Arabs but Berbers, or at least of Berber descent. Of course, many have become "Arabised", but 35% of the Algerians speak Berber as their native language. One of the most amazing sights in Algiers were the street cars, in which we could often find sheep and goats travelling with human beings. We were not allowed to use street cars, but trolley buses were not out of bounds.

On Sunday 20th December we were sent on detachment from La Redoute to Birmandries, several miles from Algiers. We were billeted beside a convent a few kilometres from the town and were on guard as soon as we arrived there. Next morning we were off duty and in the afternoon went into town on a Yankee jeep and bought a few things and had a few drinks. On our return to camp we found that my two pals, Cameron and Hipson, were on posting to the Forward Area. I spoke to the Platoon Officer and was finally allowed to go with them. We were taken in a truck to the Zoological Gardens, once more, where we joined most of the other blokes who had come with us to the 931 G.T. Coy from La Perouse. About midnight we were put on lorries and sent back to La Perouse, where the first thing we did was to sign a form certifying that we had "been warned for service in the Forward Area." My pals and I were given a tent to spend the night in, and after eating some tinned food we had "scrounged" while working at the Algiers docks we got into bed about 2 a.m.

We were called up at 4.30 a.m., had a snack for breakfast, and fell in in marching order in our draft (there were 4 drafts all told). We marched about 15 kilometres to Rouiba, and came to a halt in the railway station. We waited here all day until about 9.30 p.m., when our train arrived, a long line of cattle trucks with a couple of carriages tacked on for officers. 30 of us piled into one cattle truck, which was to be our home for 4 nights and 3 days. We didn't relish the idea when we first boarded the truck, but when the end of the journey came we were sorry to leave. Our worst trouble was getting comfortably stretched out on the floor at night, although the movement of the train did not prevent us from sleeping. We cooked our own food by means of burning wood in a biscuit tin punctured with holes. Also on the train was a company of Tiralleurs Algerians, or Moroccan infantry, with whom we used to swap tea for Vin Rouge.

The scenery and the country we passed through on this run was ever-changing, and I saw some of the most magnificent landscapes I ever set eyes on. At first we crossed undulating, fertile plains, then climbed into a wild, massive ridge of the Atlas Mountains. After the climb came the plateau, a vast barren wasteland of rocks, scrubland, cactus, and baked desert. Then we gradually dropped down into the valleys of the Algerian-Tunisian border. We had no map with which to follow our route, but I took a note of all the stations we passed through in daylight. At night the train never seemed to move more than about 20 miles. Starting from Rouiba we passed through Les Portes de Fers, Mzita, and Mansourah, where I had my first cup of black French coffee from a Red Cross Hut, and it was very good too. Then we went on through El Achir, Bordj-bou-Arreridj, El Annassen, El Hammam, and Ouled-Rhamoun, the junction for Bone and Constantine. The next two stops were

Kroubs and Bou Nouera. The train spent about an hour shunting backwards and forwards between these two stations, and we could quite easily jump out and walk along beside the train while it was moving and visit another truck if we wanted to.

During this period of shunting, a remarkable incident took place. We noticed a waggon on the next line loaded up with barrels of beer, and several fellows came out with mugs to fill up. This went on for some time, and then they began to unload the truck and roll the barrels along to our own waggons. Soon every waggon in our train had a beer-barrel in it, and as it was December 24th we contemplated having a good Xmas Eve. However, the French stationmaster was getting frantic, and it was reported to the R.T.O., who ordered all the barrels to be returned. We filled our mugs and returned our barrels, then the R.T.O. carried out a search. He found one of the barrels still concealed in a truck, and lost his temper, kicking over the men's dinner which they had cooking on a fire. One of the lads lashed out and put him on his back, and things looked as if they might take an ugly turn, but after that the affair seemed to fizzle out.

Continuing the journey, we passed through Ain-Abid, Ain-Regada, Oued-Zenata, where we saw camels for the first time, and Bourdj-Sabbath, where we were besieged by a crowd of "Wogs" selling eggs. Next came Taya, Guelma, and finally Souk-Ahras.

On the morning of 25th December we de-trained and marched 12 kilometres to an infantry transit camp at Zarouria in the mountains. We stayed here for the week-end, and the only thing of note that took place was that I did not do a guard at this camp. One amusing point was that the complete Ack-Ack defence at this camp was a set of twin Bren Guns with no ammunition!

On 27th December we travelled in lorries to Souk-Ahras and entrained once more. This trip took us through the night by Ain-Sennou, Laverdure, Ain-Araf, Ain-Tahamimime, Medjez-Safa, and Duvivier to Guelma. We de-trained at Guelma and marched 5 kilos to Millessimo, where we found ourselves once more in No.1 G.B.D., camped in the landing fields of an uncompleted aerodrome.

Our stay at this camp lasted a week, which was quite long enough as we had to put up with another dose of training and the usual "bullshit". On two occasions we walked into Guelma in the evening and had a fine dinner for 22 francs, one at the Hotel Royal and the other at the Grand Hotel. One of these occasions was New Year's Eve, and we were glad to be able to celebrate a little. On our return to camp that night we all went to bed peacefully until one of the fellows found a two-foot lizard in his blankets and we had a lively chase round the tent with mallets and bayonets.

One of the fellows at this camp, a Scotchman, managed to get drunk on New Year's Day, and for some reason was subsequently put in the guard room with a charge against him. While he was still under the influence he had an encounter with the R.S.M., and later on in the day he came reeling out of his "cell" threatening to bash the R.S.M's face in, until one of the sentries struck him on the head with his rifle-butt and laid him out. Most of the camp saw all this and were roused into little short of a mutiny, and the sentry concerned was lucky to escape being set upon by a large number of men, although he protested that he had only acted under direct orders. Over two years after I met the fellow, Len Parker by name, as a L/Cpl in my own unit.

On 7th January, 1943, at about 8 p.m. we marched off from Millessimo to Guelma and entrained once more. This time we were in a passenger coach, but found it not as comfortable as a cattle truck; the seats were hard, there was no glass in the windows, and we couldn't light a fire inside. We travelled via Souk-Ahras, Duvivier, Oued-Mougras (where we met a train of airborne troops on their way back after the first unsuccessful attempt to occupy Tunis), and Sidi-el-Messih to Ghardimaou, the frontier station between Algeria and Tunisia, which we reached on the morning of 9th January. Here about 30 of us were separated from the rest of the troops on the train, and under the command of two lieutenants, Killsby and Thomas, were told we were on draft to 78th Division and were to remain in Ghardimaou instead of going with the rest of the G.B.D. to its new location, which was a great relief to all of us.

We slept for one night in an open shed beside an Arab farm, and on the following day billeted ourselves in the disused Customs Office in the station. We had three glorious days in station, having a fine easy time and solving the food problem by pinching boxes of rations from the supply trains passing through the station. On January 13th we left Ghardimaou and again travelled by train through Oued-Meliz, Schemtou, and Sidi Meskine to Souk-el-Arba. We de-trained in the goods yard here and had hardly got all our kit off the train when we had our first taste of "enemy action." About 20 German bombers appeared overhead flying in perfect formation. We didn't realise they were Jerries until the Ack-Ack started going up, and then we hardly had time to get under cover before the bombs started dropping. About five bombs fell in the goods station, two of them couldn't have been more than 30 yards from where we were lying under some trucks. In a few minutes it was all over and none of us were hurt, but we were glad when a lorry eventually arrived and took us to an infantry transit camp a few miles from the town. We could see tracers going up in the distance for some time after that, and later I discovered that Souk-el-Arba, being a Railhead, was a favourite target for the Luftwaffe in those days.

The raid on Souk-el-Arba had scarcely finished when a thunderstorm developed and came in our direction, and Cameron and I had just managed to erect our bivouac on hard ground and get our kit under cover when the rain started. Several of the fellows were washed out during the night or had their tents blown away by the wind, but we had quite a comfortable night. It was here, however, that I first noticed how Cameron's nerves were in a bad way. The bombing had upset him considerably, and the thunder and lightning seemed to make matters worse.

Next morning, we were picked up after breakfast by a 3-ton waggon and set off to join our new company. It should have been a 30-mile run or so, but the direct road to our destination, known as "Messerschmidt Alley" was under continual strafing and considered unsuitable for troop-carrying vehicles. So we got on to a road which took us through Le Kef to Teboursouk, arrived there at dinner time, then went over the mountain road past Thibar and Sidi Smail to Beja. Here we reported to 11th Infantry Brigade Coy., R.A.S.C., but they had received reinforcements the previous night and sent us on to 78th Div. Troops Coy., where we were accepted, and remained at their H.Q. Platoon's location, in a farmhouse, for the next three days. I heard a very funny "howler" here. The French farmer and his family occupied the main building of the farm, and somebody must have objected to the troops lounging about on the veran-dah at dinner-time, for one morning the M.S.M. held a parade on which he told us there was "to be no corrugating about the farandula!"

Eventually we were split up and sent to different platoons, and I found myself in B Transport Platoon.

THE LONG WINTER

At this point it may be as well to note that the famous British 1st Army was at this time represented in the Tunisian battle area by one Infantry Division, the 78th, holding a front which stretched almost 100 miles from Sedjenane in the North to El Aroussa in the South, which I think must be the longest, or at least one of the longest, front lines ever held by one division. Units of the 6th Armoured Div. had been landing at Bone since the end of December '42, and were in action in a northern sector, but their tanks were very much inferior in numbers to Von Arnim's armour. The 78th Div. consisted of two infantry brigades, the 11th and 36th, plus the 1st Guards Brigade and a Commando unit. So acute was the shortage of fighting men that the Paratroop battalion who had made the original airborne landings were now being used in the line as infantry. The "Hot Spot" of the whole front seemed to be the village of Medjez-El-Bab and its railway station, with the surrounding ridges and valleys. "Longstop Hill" was the name given to a mountain ridge north-east of Medjez which was the scene of continual bitter fighting, and further north-east was "Banana Ridge", another bloody battle-ground which changed hands time and time again during the campaign. A battalion of the Hampshire Regt. was massacred in the Medjerola valley after a magnificently heroic stand against the relentless German infantry and Panzer attacks. The small town of Tebourba had also changed hands two or three times during the battle which took place during the first British attempt to effect an early advance into Tunis city. On one occasion my own company had delivered rations and ammunition to newly-formed dumps in the main street of Tebourba, and two hours later all the supplies fell into the hands of the attacking German infantry. During the British retreat which followed the incident, R.A.S.C. drivers had wandered for days in the hills, mapless and compassless, making their way back to their company lines and avoiding the German-held main roads.

At the time when I joined my unit, the 36th Inf.Bde. held the northern sector round Sedjenane and Mateur, while the Medjez salient was held by the 11th Inf.Bde and 1st Guards Bde. Further south on the Goubellat plain were some of the 6th Armoured Div, and close to them on the hills round Bau Arada were British parachutists and a battalion of the French Foreign Legion. About this time also (mid-January, 1943) the 38th (Irish) Inf.Bde. was arriving to join the division and replace the independent 1st Guards Bde, which in February made a forced march south to the Kasserine Pass, where the American army under the command of the greatly overrated General Patton were in headlong retreat. The "picture" at the time I joined the unit was therefore one of constant uncertainty, and although we were several miles behind the front line stand-to was the order at dawn every morning, and guards went on duty in twos with loaded rifles and "one up the spout."

For my first night in B platoon I was bivouacked in a sloping field beside a stream, then on the following morning we moved up into a farm. I was detailed as second driver to a 3-ton Bedford, and our duties were mostly routine work, although everything had to be done at night as Jerry's Focke-Wolfs and Messerschmidts had the roads covered almost all day long, and the R.A.F. were totally absent except when one or two Spitfires would venture out from the airfield at Souk-el-Arba, where we had one badly battered and depleted squadron.

"Dog-fights" took place pretty frequently over our heads, but our fighters were usually outnumbered by the Luftwaffe. The infantry in the line had not a scrap of air support until the very end of the campaign, as our fighter 'drome at Souk-el-Arba was too far back and suffering from a disgusting shortage of planes and petrol. The nearest bomber 'drome was at Algiers. American Flying Fortress formations did occasionally pass over us on their way to bomb the German rear areas, but on one fateful day they bombed Souk-el-Arba in error and inflicted many casualties on our own troops in the town.

One of my first jobs was to go in a convoy to Sidi Smail, the railhead where "pack trains" were off-loaded, and collect Compo rations for issue to the division. We set off at dusk, and an hour and a half's driving brought us to Sidi Smail after dark. The pack train, as usual, was late and it was almost midnight when we started loading. We had not been very long on the job when a warning of aircraft overhead was given. They passed over us, but in a few minutes distant explosions and Ack-Ack fire indicated that Jerry was once again bombing the Souk-el-Arba airfield and railway station. We were ready to dive for cover when we heard them coming back and we were wise to do so for at least one plane had decided that we were worth having a pot at and machine-gun bullets rattled like hailstones on the roofs of the station buildings and railway wagons. Fortunately they had already got rid of all their bombs. We could not switch on a single light on our trucks and very dim hurricane lamps were used inside the railway wagons during the offloading, but the engine of the train maintained a blazing coal fire all the time and made all our precautions seem rather pointless.

On the following night the same lorries which had loaded up petrol and rations from Sidi Smail and Souk-el-Arba were on Supply Point duty on the outskirts of Beja, where units drew their rations, and this routine was kept up during the two weeks that we stayed in this location. They passed fairly uneventfully, except for one amusing incident. I was on guard one night and was sitting in the guard room having supper when we heard some shouting some distance away in the glen at the back of the farm. The first thought which occurred to everyone, of course, was that either German parachutists had dropped in the area or a long-distance patrol had penetrated our lines and was creeping up on us. Rifles and Tommy-guns were grabbed, every available man was called out and we were ordered to spread out round the farm, while the guard commander and two guards ventured forth into the night to see what was doing. Not long after they returned, bringing with them an old Arab gentleman, who had been doing all the shouting. Seemingly he and his family were refugees from the battle area and were journeying on foot to Beja where they had some friends. He had lost his family and his way, and was wandering about the hills until long after 6 o'clock the prevailing curfew. So we gave him some biscuits, locked him up in a shed, and sent him on his way again the following morning.

There was another incident, not quite as funny. One morning an Arab farm worker was found pinching a petrol can, and our officer Capt. Butcher decided it would be worthwhile having a look round the Arab huts to see what else they might have. The Arab settlement was about 300 yards away at the rear of the farm, and Capt. Butcher and the French farmer went down and carried out a search. They found quantities of Army clothing, petrol cans both empty and full, camouflage nets for lorries, etc., and we could see the farmer freely using his horse-whip amongst the culprits. They were all brought up to the farm, some of them being small Arab boys of 8 or 10 years of age, and when we saw him lashing them with his whip most of the fellows got mad and protested vigorously, some of them on the point of striking the farmer. At this point our Padre put in a timely appearance and we explained to him that we didn't like to see children being horse-whipped, even if they were Arabs. He agreed it was not human, but said we could do nothing as the French law permitted it. We were unwise to interfere, as we did not know how to deal with Arabs, and what seemed inhuman to us was not regarded nearly as seriously either by the Arabs or the French. The conclusion of the affair was that Arab police-men came up from Beja that afternoon and officially horse-whipped three men, fathers of the children who had done the thieving. It was a typical example of the hatred existing between the Arabs and their French masters. Later that day I was talking to Paulette, a girl from Paris who had lived on the farm since the outbreak of war, and she summed up the French point of view in this way:- "An Arab will first of all steal your money; the next day he will steal your clothes; and the next day he will stick a knife in your back!"

On the 3rd of February we were scheduled for a move, and at 2:30 a.m. we were awakened, packed up, loaded the lorries and moved off at 4.15 a.m. We passed through Souk-el-Khemis once again, and over the mountain road through Thibar to Teboursouk, where the company moved into an olive grove by the side of the road to Medjez-el-Bab. Bivouacs were brought out again, and we scattered under the trees. Shortly after our arrival in this new location I was detached and subsequently posted to Composite Platoon, the supply platoon, as driver of the "G1098" waggon, i.e. the lorry which carried all the platoon's equipment, such as tents, tarpaulins, marquees, tables, etc. Theoretically this meant that I should only need to take my lorry out of the location when the entire platoon moved, but the shortage of men made this impossible and I often had to go on details with the transport platoons. The rest of the time I lent a hand issuing rations or petrol on the supply points.

From the first day of our arrival in Teboursouk the weather took a turn for the worse. It rained almost every day for weeks on end, so that dry blankets and clean clothes became a thing of the past. Boots were never anything else but sodden, battle-dresses were caked with mud and blankets hung out to dry on every occasion that the sun put in a brief appearance. A typical example of the trying conditions was on the night of February 10th, when Cameron and I were on guard. The rain was torrential all night, and when we came off duty at six in the morning we found the usual large pool of water outside our bivvy. We decided to clear it away after breakfast but when we returned from the cookhouse we found that the pool had shifted to the inside of the tent and the water was about 4ins. deep in the pit we had dug to make more room for ourselves. Our entire kits were soaked through, of course, and we had to find a new place for our tent. This is only one example of what happened only too often. No amount of moat-digging could protect the bivvies from the Tunisian rain.

My first taste of shell-fire was one night when I delivered a load of compo boxes and Tommy Cookers to Medjez-el-Bab station. I was shaking with fear, although other fellows there who had had the experience more often than they could remember showed no signs of emotion whatsoever. Bombing was not new to me, but the whine of Jerry's 88s sent shivers up and down my spine. Before the Tunisian campaign had finished I too had learned to live under fire as if nothing unusual was going on, but there were many times when one felt that peculiar feeling in the stomach, even towards the end of the war.

About two weeks after the first trip to Medjez I went with an "A" Platoon convoy carrying 25-pounder shells to an R.A. battery at Toukabeur, some distance beyond Medjez. While we were unloading, with Jerry's shells passing safely over our heads all the time, we suddenly came under a heavy mortar bombardment. Jerry was apparently trying to "stonk" our infantry who were about a mile ahead of us at the foothills of "Banana Ridge", but the Hun must have over-estimated the distance and his "Sobbing Sisters", or Nebelwerfer shells, were landing near our artillery lines. We were only on the edge of the bombardment, which lasted about 45 minutes, but it was bad enough. The unloading was stopped and we "got down to it" in ditches and slit trenches until things got a bit quieter. Three lorries had their canopies torn with shrapnel, and one had a windscreen smashed, but there were no casualties. After that, shellfire seemed easier to put up with.

During our stay in the Teboursouk location I made about four runs to Medjez-el-Bab, but no more to Toukabeur for which I was thankful. I made several trips to supply points at Testour and Sloughia helping the issuers to issue rations. Every available man was needed for this job now so in the middle of February comps rationing ceased and bulk rations came on the menu, a thing which our men had never experienced before.

For two days we had the 18th Infantry Regt., U.S. Army camped behind us, and a lot of mutual entertainment went on. I happened to mention for some reason to one of the G.Is that I had run out of toothpaste, and he gave me a box with 12 tins in it. That's the way the Yanks do things. What did shake us was their Ack-Ack equipment. Every morning we were awakened regularly about 6.30 with the spasmodic gunfire which greeted two Messerschmidts ("Mutt and Jeff") who flew all around the area. But the first morning that the Yanks were there we were practically blasted out of our blankets by the terrific burst of Ack-Ack fire all round us, making our twin Bren guns sound like toys.

After the Yanks we had a company of Moroccan muleteers beside us for a couple of days, who with their horses, mules and carts provided an amusing contrast to our mechanical transport.

About the 20th of February the Germans attacked all along the line. The strongest attack was in the south at the Kasserine Pass, where the Americans were forced to retreat. But there was also quite a serious break-through in our own lines at a point known as "Tally-ho Corner", south-west of Medjez. Here Jerry turned north and was sending his tanks and infantry to attack Medjez from the rear, and if he had succeeded things would have looked pretty grim for us. All available men in our company were rounded up, leaving the minimum number of men behind to drive our lorries back to Souk-el-Arba if the necessity should arise. With about 45 others I paraded in battle order and we were taken in two lorries to Medjez, where we joined some other fellows from the divisional R.A.S.C. companies. We took over from a reserve coy. of the Irish Guards who were being sent into the front line. Apparently we were meant to defend Medjez station if Jerry got this far, but fortunately we were never called upon to do so. His advance parties actually came within two or three miles from Medjez but were beaten off by the M.Ps of the Div Provo. Coy at a point which became known as "Redcap Alley", and the whole attacking force was routed within two days.

Another night the news came round that parachutists had been dropped in the Teboursouk area and we were called out on a patrol, but of course nothing happened. It was one of the few dry, clear nights and I expect somebody got the wind up and started a rumour.

While we were in this location the area was machine-gunned two or three times, which was not very often considering that Jerry's aircraft passed over practically every day and every night. Only once was a bomb dropped, and it landed in the middle of the town killing one or two Arabs. By this time my pal Cameron had gone into hospital suffering from his nerves. We had about seven weeks at Teboursouk, with various spells of excitement when our duties took us to Medjez or when the unopposed Luftwaffe spotted us, but the worst feature of life at this time was the eternal rain and thunderstorms which made our camp a miserable place to live in. We were therefore not sorry when we learned that the division was coming out of the line for a short rest, and about 8 o'clock in the evening on 23rd March the whole company moved out of the olive grove and headed down the road to Le Kef. Before the road actually came into Le Kef we turned right and followed a rough track, only just wide enough to accommodate 3-ton vehicles, for several miles into the mountains. We stopped about 1 a.m., and as it was fortunately a fine night we slept in the open under the trees.

All the divisional R.A.S.C. companies were camped in the surrounding woods, and the whole division was located within a radius of a few miles except for one Brigade who had stayed nearer the forward area. For us there was not a great deal of rest or recreation, as the division had to be fed whether it was in the line or out of it, but every man received in return 48 hrs. free of duty which was highly acceptable. There was nowhere to go, of course, but it was nice to lie in bed in the morning. For the first seven days we had plenty of sunshine with only occasional showers of rain and we began to feel as if winter was actually being left behind at last. On our first Saturday evening here a company concert was held, attended by our C.,R.A.S.C, Lt/Col. Hart, and it produced a lot of good talent amongst the fellows. While we were here Cameron came back from hospital but his nervous state had not improved. If anything he had got worse in the C.C.S. at bomb-shattered Souk-el-Arba, and decided he could face life better amongst his friends in the unit, but it was not long before he was taken away again.

Our period of "rest", however, proved to be short-lived as the newly-arrived 1st. Division, who had relieved our infantry in the line, were having a bad time and our battalions were recalled. On the night of 2nd April we moved out once again and pulled in once more at Teboursouk, in a different location to the last one but under the same familiar olive trees. On our second night here we came in for the worst night air raid we had experienced yet. It didn't last longer than about half an hour, but while it lasted the whole sky was aflame with flares, tracer bullets and the star-like flashes of bursting Ack-Ack shells. Many bombs were dropped, but luckily none of them landed in our location. We had not yet dug any slit trenches, and we felt terribly exposed lying on the ground or in shallow ditches.

A few miles to the west of Teboursouk a new ammunition dump had been formed near the ruins of an ancient Roman town called Dougga, and the first time I went to this dump on duty I took the opportunity of spending over an hour having a look at the ruins. An elderly Frenchman showed me round and explained the different items. It was built about 200 years B.C., and the whole town was in an extremely good state of preservation. The outstanding features were the Amphitheatre, the Forum, the Baths, the Temple of Jupiter, the Slave Market, and, curiously enough, the Public Latrines. The most interesting of these was the Temple, where there were several beautiful mosaics and a huge sun-dial on the floor.

We spent two weeks at this location, then on 18th April we moved out of Teboursouk once again, this time for good. We climbed the mountain road to Souk-el-Khemis, and in about an hour's time arrived at our new camp on the left of the road between Thibar and Sidi Smail. The lorries parked up in scattered positions over the flat, open fields which stretched for miles around us, offering no camouflage whatsoever. It was about 5 o'clock on a fine afternoon, and it didn't surprise us in the least when, a few minutes after our arrival, five Messerschmidts came in from the east and started "straffing" the whole length of the road. We were lucky to be only a few miles from Souk-el-Arba airfield, for as we lay in the long grass hoping for the best we saw four Spitfires streaking in amongst the M.Es. The usual dog-fights took place, and this time it wasn't long before three M.Es were shot down and the other two turned tail and fled.

There was quite a lot of air activity over our heads while we were here, but fortunately our stay only lasted six days. The day before we moved again a company parade was held and our O.C., Major C.W.S. Broadbent, gave us a lecture and explained our rather puzzling moves. The final drive for Tunis was due to begin very soon, and at the present time the division was re-grouping and moving its position in the line. All the R.A.S.C. was concentrated in this rear zone of the forward area, and on the following day we were moving up again to our new locations, which would be our last move before the fall of Tunis. Preparations had been made to make us highly mobile, such as the withdrawal of bivouacs and two blankets from each man. We were now to sleep completely in the open, and we were glad that for the time being at least there was no rain, although the nights were still pretty cold and in the early morning our kits were wet with dew.

A peculiar thing happened on 24th April, the morning of our move. Reveille was at 4 a.m. as we had to be ready for moving off at 6 a.m. Exactly at 4 o'clock a lone German plane came over and dropped one bomb in a field about 400 yards from our location, and it was the most successful method I've ever seen of getting an entire company out of bed on the dot at Reveille! At six o'clock we pulled out and passed through Beja and Oued Zarga to another open location on a hillside near the artillery lines in the region of Toukabeur.

That afternoon the location was twice machine-gunned from the air, and during the first night bombs were dropped on the road about half a mile away. Cameron's nerve gave way completely here and on the following morning he was admitted into hospital as a neurotic case and we never saw him again. From this location I went on two or three details carrying petrol to a huge petrol dump which a small detachment of our issuers was establishing just south of Medjez. It was to be used as a filling station for tanks in the tank battle which was expected to precede the final advance into Tunis. During this time bitter fighting had been going on in Banana Ridge, and all night long on every night for about a week the sky was bright with continuous gunflashes and the ground quivered with the periodical salvoes when every gun in the line seemed to go off at the same instant. The 78th Div. was no longer alone in the battle now, as we were flanked by the 1st and 4th Infantry Divisions and the 46th Indian Div, which had come over from the 8th Army to take part in the 1st Army's push for Tunis. About the beginning of May also the R.A.F. started to show itself in strength, and it did our hearts good to see, for the first time in this campaign, wave after wave of bombers and fighters passing over us to bomb the Germans' roads, troop concentrations, supply dumps etc. The weather by now was beautiful, and on the 1st of May we were issued with our Khaki Drill, and we knew that winter was at last a thing of the past. Mosquito-nets came into use, and instructional lectures were given on anti-malaria precautions. It was fine to sleep in the open at night with only the thin nets over us, and even with only two blankets no-one felt cold. It was a pleasure to get up at Reveillé, and to wash stripped to the waist in the open, to have dry bedding and clean kits.

The last great attack began on 7th May, and between two and three o'clock in the morning we were awakened by the colossal artillery barrage. It was fascinating to watch; the whole sky to the east was a blaze of continuous light; it was impossible to distinguish individual gunflashes, and the whole horizon was like a quivering, undying, white glow.

On Saturday 8th May the whole company moved to Medjez, and camped for the night off the road to the south of the battered and ruined town. Fighting was now taking place in the streets of Tunis and Bizerta and, by the following morning, both these places had fallen. So on the morning of the 9th I had just come off guard when the order came to move again. We passed through Medjez again and joined the long, seemingly endless convoy of lorries, armoured cars, staff cars and vehicles of every description heading for Tunis. Before long we met the beginning of a similar convoy coming down the other side of the road from Tunis, waggon after waggon of assorted Germans and Italians going back to the P.O.W. cages which had been hastily set up in the rear. The going was painfully slow, and fellows were leaning over from our trucks and handing packets of cigarettes to the Germans, who were exchanging watches, binoculars, compasses, and anything else they could get rid of. There were 3-ton lorries with about 40 men in each, 6-tonners carrying God knows how many men, and German vehicles with German drivers following the convoy back to the cages. Guards were not to be seen, but these Jerries and "Ities" knew there was nothing for it but to accept the hospitality of British P.O.W. camps. At Massicault we met a column of marching Germans, some with full kits and some with nothing at all, but all looking utterly exhausted, making their way back. It was a wonderful sight, and made one feel rewarded for the miseries of the past six months.

From Massicault we went on through Bordj-el-Amri and St. Cyprien to La Mornaghia, a village about 10 miles from Tunis where we camped on the fringes of wide, flat fields along the sides of the dusty road. The campaign was over, and the theme-song now was "Where do we go from here?"

TUNIS AND THE "SUMMER HOLIDAYS"

A few days after the wind-up of the campaign an order-of-the-day was published at G.H.Q. and circulated amongst the units of the Brit. 1st Army, in which General Anderson congratulated and thanked his troops for services rendered, and also reminded them that this was only the first step in the defeat of the Axis. "After the briefest of pauses", he said, we would be meeting the "Herrenwolk" again. As far as the 78th Div. was concerned the pause actually lasted for two months, during which we basked in the beautiful North African summer, bathed in the cool, buoyant waters of the Mediterranean, and made ourselves at home in the city of Tunis.

On May 15th we had our first platoon binge, which coincided very nicely with my 20th birthday. We purchased several gallons of vin rouge from a local farmer, which we drank along with a substantial quantity of buckshee army rum. On May 17th I had my first day pass into Tunis. To enter Tunis from the west you pass through the great arch known as the Bab-el-Khadra, or "Green Gate", and then after passing the Bardo, ancient and impressive palace of the Bey of Tunis, you come into the city itself. I found it a much cleaner town than Algiers with wider streets and more modern buildings. The Avenue Jules Ferry, the "Broadway" of Tunis, stretches from the sea to the inland end of the European part of the town, where an arch called the Porte de France divides the modern quarter from the Arab quarter. We spent quite a lot of time wandering about the Arab quarter, which was of course much the same as the Kasbah of Algiers except that it was more or less level instead of rising in steps, and there was more stuff on sale in the "souks", or bazaars. The "Souk of Perfumes" in Tunis is world-famous, and as each "souk" has its own particular goods on the market you have the Souk of Saddlers, the Souk of Fruit, etc. For the first time I was able to see a minaret, the tall, white tower which is to be found in all Muslim towns and from which the "muezzin" calls the faithful to prayer at sunrise, noon, and sunset.

On our first day in Tunis we found a small school on the outskirts of the town run by some English ladies, who had been there throughout the German occupation. They told us a lot of interesting stories about life in Tunis during the previous six months, and took us round to St. George's Church, which stands on a piece of consecrated British ground, and over which the French authorities have no control. At the time when the slave traffic was still practised in N. Africa it provided sanctuary for any escaped slave who came into the grounds. Having once been in, a slave could go out again a free man. In the graveyard of St. George's Church I saw the grave of John Howard Payne, who wrote the song "Home, Sweet Home." He was an Englishman on the staff of the American consulate in Tunis, and wrote the song at Constantine.

On May 20th I went to Tunis again and watched the colourful Victory Parade as it passed along the Avenue Gambetta, and also managed to buy a bottle of the finest Muscatel wine from a French hotel manager who had been some years in London.

The Avenue Jules Ferry continues into the sea as a dike or mole along which trolley-cars travel to and from Carthage across the bay called "El Bahira", or "The Little Sea", and we went there a couple of times on swimming parties. Regular swimming parties were also run to Sidi-bou-Said and Sainte Germaine, on the Gulf of Tunis.

One of our biggest enjoyments on these visits to Tunis was the opportunity to go once again to the pictures, after such a long time without even seeing a cinema. I also went one evening to a very good French variety show at the Théâtre de la Chanson, "Le Petit Théâtre de L'Elite."

About the end of May we were all surprised to hear that the division was moving back to Algeria for "rest and training", and as we didn't see why we couldn't rest and train in our present area everybody came to the conclusion that we were being sent back to England. Anyway, on the morning of May 30th we left La Mornaghia, passing through Djedeida and Chaouat, where we saw many signs of the recent battles and had to drive over several diversions off the shell-holed main roads. From Sidi Athman and Ain Rhelal we went on to Mateur, which did not seem to be knocked about much. We halted for lunch in the flat country around Michaud and then moved on into the mountains on bad surface roads. All the surrounding hillsides and fields were still being examined by American engineers for mines, and shell-holes, bomb craters, dug-outs, etc, were in evidence everywhere. We passed through battered and ruined

Sedjenane, and then started going downhill once more on to what seemed to be a patch of desert, which looked strangely out of place in this verdant country. As the plains began we came on to good roads again, and we were soon in sight of the sea again at Lacroix, where we saw a peninsular hill, reminiscent of Dumbarton Rock, jutting out from the mainland with a very impressive castle or fort on the summit.

We camped for the night near Roume-es-Souk, and on the following morning we set off again into the mountains, passing through Blandan and Lac des Oiseaux into Algeria. In the afternoon we eventually came on to the Guelma road, but throughout the morning progress was very slow in the hills, specially as we ran into streams of traffic, mostly American, coming in the opposite direction. With the whole division on the move at the same time our convoy must have been a terrific size. At one point we had halted for a few minutes and the traffic on the other side of the road was also more or less stationary, when a Yankee driver called over to me "Say, what outfit's this with the hatchet sign on their trucks?" I told him it was 78th Division, and he said "Well, it sure is a big one. They've been holding me up all the way from Goddam Constantine!"

Once on the Guelma road it was not long before we had passed the little railway station called Petit and arrived at Millessimo, which seemed to be greatly increased in its population since the last time I was here when there was hardly a soul to be seen. Our new company location was the same group of fields round the hangar where I had spent New Year's week with No. 1 G.B.D. This time we were here for three weeks having a fairly easy life, except that being pretty far inland the heat was stifling, and we longed to get back to the sea coast again. The most popular form of recreation here was swimming, and we took every chance we could to go to the Roman Baths of Heliopolis. This was a circular pool about 30 yards in diameter and about 4 and a half feet deep all round. The water was almost warm and it was a joy to bathe in it. We went to Guelma now and again, but there was no place to go except the NAAFI, unless you wanted to look at the old Roman wall.

On the 17th we lined the route for the King when he arrived at Guelma on his N. African tour. He looked tired and worried as he stood in his car saluting.

One night we were struck by a Sirocco wind, a violent, hot wind which blew down every tent in the camp, swept mosquito-nets away like bits of fluff and scattered everybody's bedding and kit in all directions. While we were at this place a large number of fellows went in hospital with dysentery and a few with malaria. On June 18th most of the company's vehicles were sent off to Oran for embarkation and hopes were high that we might be going home, but on the 20th the rest of the company started off back into Tunisia, and by the time we had reached Beja, our first stop, we began to think that we would be sailing for a different destination. The next day we passed through Tunis and headed south to a point a few miles from the village of Grombalia, where we parked in an olive grove amongst a lot of derelict Italian armoured cars and abandoned equipment, including small stacks of dum-dum bullets which the Italians were noted for using frequently during the desert campaign. Since most our transport had left us we had ceased to be an operational unit, and consequently had an easy time. We went swimming every afternoon at a seaside place called Bordj-Cedria, where there was a fine beach.

One morning I was looking for a place to wash some clothes when I came across a well which the local Arab farmer used for irrigating his land. Two large buckets, or containers, made of tough hide, were lowered into the well and pulled up by two camels, then they were emptied into a trough and the water flowed out into a little channel and all round the fields. The camels kept this up all morning, patiently walking backwards and forwards, but this afternoon when we went up to do some washing they were having a siesta. We had to do our own hauling, and it was as much as three of us could do to pull one container at a time. The Arab farmer was a very intelligent sort of fellow and interesting to talk to. He told us two curious points about camels, that they are contaminated with syphilis more than any other animal (which makes their bite very dangerous), and that they cannot swim, for their heads are so awkwardly placed that they turn over very easily and drown.

While we were at Grombalia we were visited by General Montgomery, who was C-in-C. 8th Army, of course, and decided the fate of our division. The whole divisional R.A.S.C. was on parade, forming three sides of a square, when Monty arrived in his car. He stood up, and having been greeted by our Colonel he looked around the parade and said "Come closer." We broke ranks and flocked round his car, and the next order was "Take your hats off." Then he looked us over again, found us all looking well, and told us we were now in the Eighth Army. He had heard all about 78th Div., and had decided that he wanted us in his Army, so now we knew that southern Europe would almost definitely be our next destination.

On Friday 9th July we moved out from our Grombalia location, and went through Enfidaville across flat country to a point about 15 miles from Sousse. This was a 'concentration area', and all passes to Tunis were stopped; Sousse was out-of-bounds, and we were now too far from the sea for swimming parties to be continued. As a substitute we went on periodical visits to a nearby Mobile Bath Unit for a shower, and to take up our time a company sports tournament was arranged, plus various programmes of P.T., lectures, debates, etc.

On July 21st we moved from this location to an olive grove a couple of hundred yards from the sea south of Sousse. Bathing here would have been splendid had it not been for the jellyfish which were in the bay in large numbers and could give a nasty sting.

On the evening of July 26th we packed up suddenly and were taken in battle order to the docks at Sousse. We lined up here facing a row of Assault Landing Craft, and about 9.30 we put on our "Mae Wests" and embarked. We went below immediately and took a bunk each. They were very comfortable spring bunks, but it was very hot in the hold and we lay down without blankets. Eventually, like the others, I dozed off and was fast asleep when the ship slipped out of the harbour in darkness and left North Africa behind.

2.   SICILY

On the morning of 27th July, '43, I awoke to find myself rocking gently from side to side on my bunk. I got up and went up on deck, where the swaying of the ship was more pronounced but the fresh air was very refreshing. There was quite a heavy sea running and the convoy of shallow-bottomed craft was being tossed about on the waves, doing about 8 or 9 knots. The ship, LCI No.305, was about 80 ft. in length and the deck about 6ft above sea level. She was American built and carried 5 Oerlikon A/A guns. After breakfast I was sick, like everybody else on the boat, and although I managed to have all the remaining meals of the day without any come-back I felt pretty rough all day. I was detailed for a 4-hour spell of duty on one of the guns aft, but after my period of duty was over I remained stretched out in the gun-pit and was still there at 10 o'clock in the evening when we all went below to our bunks. That afternoon we passed the island of Limosa, and during the night we left Malta behind. On the following morning the sea was fine and calm, and we could see the coast of Sicily faintly outlined on the horizon. About noon we entered the busy harbour of Avola, about 15 miles south of Syracuse, and we were all on deck with our kits eager to disembark. The initial landings of the invasion of Sicily had taken place about six or seven days ago, and the beach at Avola was a hive of industry. The bay was full of ships of every description, from cruisers and destroyers to LCIs and tramp steamers. While we were still waiting to land two planes zoomed low across the bay machine-gunning all the way and disappeared just as suddenly into the blue.

About two o'clock we disembarked, and sat around on the beach for a while. We found some grape vines and were not long in sampling the juicy, black grapes which are to be found everywhere in Sicily. About 30 minutes later we marched off into our first experience of the enemy's home ground, and after 3 miles or so we reached the Div. Assembly Area, where we pitched our bivvies. Here we rejoined the transport sections who had left us at Guelma and who had arrived here the previous day. I was on guard that night, and shortly after midnight enemy planes started coming over and attacking the Bay and the nearby airstrip. A terrific barrage was put up by the ships, and although there was no bombing in our area we had to dive under lorries to avoid the showers of falling shrapnel.

Next morning there was a parade, after which I washed some K.D. and other clothes, but they were still wet when we were told to pack up and be ready to move off on an advance party at 10 a.m. Eight of us piled into a waggon full of kit and joined a convoy of one of our sister R.A.S.C. companies who were moving up to our new operational area. We travelled through the Sicilian countryside, not unlike that of Tunisia, and over a range of mountains, passing through little villages, dirty and with narrow streets, and full of loitering civilians. Kids threw lemons at us and asked for cigarettes and biscuits. The men seemed to be desperate for fags, and we were soon to find out that cigarettes would become the most popular form of currency in "business deals" with the Italians. We went through Palazzolo, Floridia, Vizzini and one or two other small places till we stopped in a nut-grove in a valley about 15 miles south of Centuripe, where our infantry was at that time held up.

On August 3rd the 38th Irish Bde. made their glorious bayonet charge up the open face of Centuripe hill and took the town at the summit, dislodging the Germans from their most formidable strong-point in the line, and the division was on the move again. We moved to a location by the side of "Moon Track", up in the hills. On our first day here we were strafed by six enemy planes, but that was the last time we saw the Luftwaffe during the brief Sicilian campaign. On Aug. 6th we moved again past Libertinia Station to a field on the Catenanuova-Catania road, where we remained till the 10th. The next move was over the mountains to Centuripe and down through the battlefields to a location on the other side of Adrano, more or less at the foot of Mount Etna.

I never had an opportunity of climbing the great volcano, but it made an impressive sight and particularly interesting were the numerous colour-changes which took place on the mountain-side at different times of the day as the sun moved round. Near this location there was an aqueduct of fast-running water flowing down towards the River Salso. There were pools in the river deep enough to swim in, but the water was terribly cold and the bottom was all rough stones. Still, the heat at this time of the year was terrific, and it was fine to have a quick dip in mid-afternoon.

By the end of August the campaign in Sicily was drawing to a close, and the Germans were being chased across the Straits of Messina to Italy. At 2 o'clock in the morning on August 28th we were roused from sleep, packed up, and left the location by four. North was the general direction, and we climbed through

Bronte and Randazzo, where Jerry had fought stiff rearguard actions and which were both badly knocked about. We still kept on climbing, reaching a height of about 2000 ft above sea level, and Mount Etna was now well behind us to the south. After Randazzo we passed through S. Domenica Vittoria, then began a long, winding run down to the coast. We passed through Raccuia where we saw the local police force or 'carabinieri'. It being Sunday, they were dressed in their colourful dress uniforms and Napoleon hats, quite a large force for such a small town. While we were coming down the mountains we came in sight of the sea and the Mediterranean really was blue when seen from our position. We had some fine views of the Lipari Islands before we eventually came onto the coast road at Patti.

We turned left and headed westwards for a few miles along this road, which, in contrast to all the other roads we had come over, bore no traces of warfare, except at one point where a wooden bridge had been thrown over a crater. It was just at the entrance to the east end of a tunnel at Capo Calavo, and as it was impossible to make a diversion off this road it looked very much as if it had been deliberately mined by the retreating enemy. Once through the tunnel it was not long before we reached Brolo, where we pulled in to the left up a valley by the side of a wide dried-up river bed. It was a good location, with plenty of trees to shade us, plenty of grapes, and only a few hundred yards from the sea, but nevertheless it was destined to give us a bit of trouble.

The petrol lorries were unloaded, and the stacks of petrol and diesel were formed all along the river bed by the side of the bivvy lines. The following morning a fierce squall, our first experience of rough weather for a couple of months, blew down some of our tents, and in the afternoon there was a sudden downpour of rain. Later on dark clouds hid the mountain-tops to the south and distant lightning indicated a storm somewhere. The outcome of this was that about 9.30 in the evening the river bed beside our camp became a raging torrent, and parties of men were sent out to salvage some of the petrol cans which were floating in scores towards the sea, along with various other items of equipment. Altogether about 900 gallons were lost, providing new headaches for the L/Cpl I/C P.O.L!

NIGHT IN MESSINA – SEPTEMBER '43

Under the blue-black hollow bowl of stars
We slept one night beside the muttering sea,
Between bomb-broken streets and the dark water
Where slept like whales the sidelong-sunken ships.

This city should be haunted by the ghosts
Of bombers which return to view their work:
The Ack-ack flower again in balls of fire
And lines of light, a million patterns there.

Beautiful as a set-piece avalanche
Of sound and rubble, graves and requiem.
The city buried by night's avalanche
Is silent, cratered, dead as the round moon.

But this delusion of the night recalls
Reality; the previous afternoon;
The dusty streets beneath the sun and all
The hawkers selling grapes and cheapjack stock,

Exacting tribute from the conquerors.
They are the common people who survive
The Avalanche, and reappear each day.
    Clifford Dobb, R.A.S.C.

The next day, however, the weather was normal again and we continued to bask in beautiful sunshine. There was plenty of swimming, and in the evenings we walked into Brolo, or further along to San Angelo. Another village we also visited was Piraino, about two miles away at the summit of a hill, but the climb was too stiff to tempt us to repeat our visit. The back streets of Brolo were very similar to the Arab quarter of Tunis, but the people were cleaner and the houses, though old, were very clean and tidy inside. We were asked into several houses, and I had my first taste here of Italian wine. Marsala was the best stuff, and it was quite plentiful here as it comes from the vineyards of Marsala, a port on the north-west coast of the island. In early times the Moors called it "Mars-al-Allah", the Harbour of God.

At this time a tremendous number of men were going down with malaria, and most of them were taken to an M.D.S. established in a monastery at Tindari, further along the coast.

The 3rd of September, besides being the fourth anniversary of the outbreak of war, was also D-Day in the invasion of Italy, and in the evening we had a church service. But it was some time before my company went into "ops" again. On the afternoon of Sept. 25th we moved out of Brolo at last and travelled along the coast road towards Messina. Several villages were passed on the way, and one apparently thriving town, Barcellona, where there were plenty of well-stocked shops. A few miles further on we left the coast road and climbed over the mountains, and it was dusk when we finally arrived in bomb-shattered Messina. We moved slowly through a maze of ruined buildings and parked the vehicles along the pavements of a street near the waterfront. After a meal I went on guard, and although the clocks were put back one hour making the guard and the night longer I had only a couple of hours in which to enjoy my bed in the gutter. Reveille was at five, and by 7 p.m. we were ready to move off.

We went through the centre of Messina, along the sunny, tree-lined main street which showed evidence of the severe aerial bombardment it had suffered. But the "ghost city" of the previous night had come to life, and the streets were crowded with people and troops. We moved down the "Lungomare" on to a beach, and subsequently each lorry embarked on an invasion barge, a fleet of which were running a ferry service across the Straits. A large board on the beach said –

YESTERDAY'S FIGURE = 702 Crossings

TODAY'S = BEAT IT!

Looking back at the fine panoramic view of Messina, we slowly approached the mainland, and after about twenty minutes we disembarked on a beach in Italy.

3.   ITALY

THE EAST COAST

We landed at about 10 a.m., 26th September 1943, on the
mainland of Italy, and from the beach we moved into a dried-up
river bed which served as a sort of marshalling-yard for newly
arrived transport. When all the unit's lorries had arrived and
the convoy was formed up we had a meal and moved off.
Passing through San Giovanni, we travelled north along the
high coast road of Calabria, from which we got some magnificent views of the coastline and the Straits. Palmi showed signs
of aerial bombardment and shelling, but there were no further
signs of fighting in any of the small villages we passed through
before reaching Cosenza. From here we turned inland and did
some stiff climbing before we finally halted at dusk and spent
the night in a wood near Catanzaro. On the following day we
struck the east coast of the "toe" of Italy at Catanzaro Marina,
and stopped for the night in a staging area near Crotone. This
part of the country was littered with pill-boxes and other
defences which had never actually been used against our
invading troops. The next day was our worst day's run; we
passed over very dusty and bumpy military roads, or roads still
under construction, and only passed through a few isolated and
unpicturesque villages, such as Curocoli and Pietropaola. At one
place a sign-board was pointing in the wrong direction (it's
possible that this was done deliberately), and the whole convoy
went up a steep hillside road, arriving at a village on the summit
which proved to be a dead end. The task of turning the vehicles

and getting back on the right road took up some time, and it was dark when we eventually camped. To make up for lost time we had to set off again at 1.30 a.m., following the coast road round the "instep" of the Italian "boot", passing through Amenclolara Oriolo and Montegiordano, and eventually arriving about noon at the famous seaport of Taranto. We stopped here only long enough to have dinner, and in the afternoon we set off again along the Via Appia, through Massafra, and stopped for the night in a field by the side of the road. On the following day, the sixth and last of our tiresome journey, we continued northwards, passing through some very attractive and thriving towns, where for the first time we were greeted in a very welcoming manner by the people in the streets. We went through Casamassima and Capurzo then came into Bari, a fine town about the size of Tunis, with well-stocked shops and several theatres, plenty of cafés and broad, sunny streets. Unfortunately we didn't stop here but went on through Giovinazzo, Molfetta, and one or two other small towns till we came to Barletta. We pulled in at an olive grove-cum-vineyard about a mile outside of the town, and this was to be our location for several days. A couple of days later we were allowed to go into the town for a few hours, and found it was a shoppers' paradise. There were any amount of first quality clothes, including silk stockings, for sale at ridiculously cheap prices. Obviously the shopkeepers had not yet got wise to the trick of charging the extortionate prices which we were met with all over Italy after the civvies had become more familiar with their "liberators". At this time the 11th Brigade were being held up by a defence force of Germans further north, and my company were called upon to issue assault supplies to the 36th Brigade, who were to make a landing further up the coast and attack Jerry from the rear. The assault force mustered at the port of Trani, and on October 4th the landings were made at Termoli. The operation was successful but casualties were fairly heavy. Major Jack Anderson of the Argylls who won the V.C. at Longstop Hill was killed, and a lot of usually non-combatant elements of the Brigade were mixed up in the fighting. Soon after this we moved out of Barletta and headed north through the village of Trinitapoli across flat "airfield" country to the ruined town of Foggia. There was nothing to be seen here except the devastation caused by our bombers when they knocked out the Foggia aerodrome and most of the town. After passing through San Severo we camped for the night, and on the following day we moved on to the next town, Serracapriola, about 15 miles away. A few miles out of this town we set up our camp, but on our first day here we experienced the worst rainstorm I have ever seen. We were thoroughly swamped out, but luckily we got accommodation for the platoon in a Franciscan monastery, the "Santuario della Madonna della Grazie", and for the first time since the days of the tennis club in Algiers I slept on a proper floor with a roof over my head. There were some interesting old characters among the monks here, one of whom became very friendly with me and doctored my neck when I developed the first of a series of boils. We had a party of Italian ex-soldiers here who were attached to us for work, and I learnt one or two Italian songs from them. We also acquired a gramophone and some old Italian records, which helped to make our billet quite a pleasant place in the evenings.

All this time we had been taking things fairly easy and enjoying glorious weather, but one day I was forcefully reminded that there was still a war on. Three of us were detailed to take an urgent supply of ammunition to the infantry on some hills further north where they were held up while Jerry was making a stand at the River Trigno. It was the Argylls once again, and it was early morning when our three lorries arrived at Battalion H.Q. As we could not move out again until dusk, we off-loaded the ammunition and helped to carry some .303 up to machine-gun posts further up the hill. The duty company was spread out on the hill, and there was nothing much doing except spasmodic shelling. Patrols were out in the valley on the other side of the hills, but as we looked down there was no sign of movement. About mid-day, however, we were having dinner with some riflemen (and pretty poor it was, too) when some shells started dropping about 100 yards in front of us. There was an immediate scatter, and everybody was getting down behind rocks and boulders. The O.P. reported four German tanks not more than three-quarters of a mile away, who had obviously spotted us and were pumping shells into our positions as hard as they could, advancing across the valley all the time. There was a chance that this might be the prelude to an attack, although in broad daylight this was hardly credible. As my pals and I were crouching on the ground, scared to death, two or three very young Argylls got up and started scurrying down the hill towards Bn.H.Q. They had only got a few yards, however, when they were confronted by a Lieutenant, who had stood up from his hollow in the ground, and faced them with a revolver in his hand. "I'll shoot the first man who takes another step this way," he said. "Now get back to your positions." Without another word they turned round and came back to where the rest of us were. By this time about 20 shells had dropped not very far in front of us, but fortunately the tanks had not judged our range accurately. 25-pounder guns about a mile away on our left had opened up on them by this time, and in a few minutes the tanks turned in their tracks and made off. Thus ended a spot of excitement with no casualties on either side.

Towards the end of October we moved from our location at the monastery, after many fond farewells from the monks, and camped in an olive grove close to the sea at Campomarino, about 15 miles further north. As soon as we took to living out in the open again the weather changed and we got several days of rain. During the next two weeks we moved in gradual stages, passing through Termoli and San Salvo, right on the coast, and then moved inland and through the larger town of Vasto. Finally we stopped near the village of Casalbordino, a couple of miles from the River Sangro, where the Germans had established their winter line of defence and where a couple of weeks later the first big battle on the east coast of Italy took place. While we were here we had constant bad weather, but fortunately we were able to use part of a farmhouse as a billet. The mud in this area was worse than anything I had ever seen in Africa. Duckboards were in use everywhere, and as they frequently disappeared under the sea of mud fellows were constantly taking a step in the wrong direction and finding themselves sunk to above the knees in it. In the fields on either side of the road could be seen scores of lorries, tanks, and Bren carriers bogged down and absolutely immovable. We were under shell-fire every day here, but fortunately nothing ever hit our location. Some of our Workshops Platoon boys had a bad break one day when they were at Div. H.Q. doing repairs on vehicles. The bombing line for our planes at this time was the

River Sangro, as all territory north of the river was in German hands and south of the river in British hands. Further south was the River Trigno, and on this occasion a flight of 12 Bostons were flying over the area, and presumably the squadron-leader or flight-lieutenant had mistaken the Trigno for the Sangro, and the 12 planes unloaded their complete cargo of bombs on Div. H.Q. and the surrounding countryside, causing many casualties and killing two of our Workshops boys. Also among the killed was Major Wright of the Argylls, who was at that time D.A.Q.M.G. in our division.

THE RIVER : 1943

You who have crossed the river,
Shed no tear
For us who made the crossing
So secure.
Our work is over in that
Vale of Fear;
Our mouths breathed curses,
But our hearts were pure.
Press bravely forward, we
Are not behind
But go before you on the
Farther side.
Having fulfilled the task to
Us assigned
To cross the river and to
Be your guide.
    8th Army News, January, 1944.

On the nights of the 27th and the 28th November the divisional artillery put up a tremendous barrage, and it was obvious that the big attack to break Jerrie's winter line was about to take place. Up to now only patrols had crossed the river, and many men had been drowned in the fast-flowing water when the rain had been heavy and the river was in flood. But on the night of the 29th the big attack went in and our infantry crossed the river in force. By dawn our admirable engineers had Bailey Bridges up, and vehicles as well as troops were able to cross. Supplies were also coming in by sea in "DUKWS", or "Ducks" as we called them, and off-loaded on the north bank of the river. As soon as the crossing had been made, however, the 2nd Canadian division came up to relieve us, and our units started to move back for a well-earned rest. On Dec.7th we moved off early in the morning, passing once again through Vasto and Termoli, then branching off inland and making for the foothills of the Appenines. We passed through Larino and Casa Calendra on the road to the large town of Campobasso, but instead of entering the latter we turned right and after a few miles came to the village of Montagno.

THE VINEYARD – DECEMBER '43

Spreading the straw upon the floor, we spread
The hopes and promises, the joys and fears,
The harvest, sometime symbol of a peace
Now trampled by the muddy boots of war.

And I remember a morning
In a ruined, shrivelled vineyard near the shore,
Where black grapes shrank, forgot by harvesters;

The seven-league shells strode high across the valley –
Continuous thunder – a spotter plane overhead ....
Then suddenly silence; and in a moment the vineyard
Was haunted, and we were alone in a hostile world.
Afterwards it was relief to work and drink
The thawing, warming tea.

Tonight the straw
Will be warm; tomorrow comes the resurrection
Of dreams; dawn brings with it a harvest of hawks;
It is our dawn, the long-awaited light.

      Clifford Dobb, R.A.S.C.

WINTER IN THE APPENINES

The company was spread out in different billets throughout the village, and my platoon was in a large building with a concrete floor and a high roof, which looked as if it had formerly been some sort of store. As we were the only unit occupying the place we soon made plenty of friends amongst the villagers, who were for the most part very amiable people, and I spent many happy evenings sitting round a civvy fire drinking "vino" or eating spaghetti.

While we were here I developed a cyst behind my left ear, which was the climax to a long succession of boils I had been having on the back of my neck ever since we were at the Serracapriola monastery. On Dec.17th I went into 7 C.C.S. at Campobasso to have it removed, but instead of cutting it they treated it with hot fomentations until it subsided. I was in hospital for 7 days and thoroughly enjoyed the rest, specially as I was allowed out in the afternoons and managed to see one or two good ENSA shows, including a show by some of Geraldo's band and his singers. On 24th Dec. I returned to the company, and that evening we "closed down" from the 25th to the 27th, which gave us the chance to have a very good Xmas holiday. We had an excellent Xmas dinner, and the canteen was open nearly all day. We went round all our Italian friends, exchanging tins of bully beef etc. for vino and vermouth, and on Boxing Day we went to see the company's first-rate Pantomime in the Teatro Savoia in Campobasso. New Year was celebrated in a quieter way, but the Scotchmen made the most of it. It was pouring wet on Hogmanay, but when we woke up on January 1st '44, we found that the rain had turned into snow, several feet of which lay on the ground, and a howling blizzard was blowing. Composite Platoon (to which I had been transferred from "B" Platoon) was due to move out on January 1st, but the move had to be postponed until January 4th when some of the roads had been partly cleared. We set off after dinner, passed through Campobasso, and headed inland for the Appenines, via Vinchiaturo and Boiano. Just before we came to Isernia we forked right and made for Pescolanciano, our ultimate destination. Here we were in good billets again, and it seemed to be quite a nice village. A surprisingly large number of the older men in the town could speak English. Life here turned out to be pretty uneventful, but there was plenty of work to do. We bought a wireless set for 5,500 lire (about £14) and it certainly helped to brighten the long winter nights. One evening I was sitting in the platoon office along with two other fellows and Capt. Eric Wilmott, all of us writing letters to start with and then the rest of us listening for about 2 hours while Capt. Wilmott told us about hiking in Germany, rowing on the Thames, and amateur theatricals. All of this time we had a charcoal brazier burning in the middle of the floor, until at 10 o'clock Capt. Wilmott went off to his billet and the rest of us got ready for bed. About 10 minutes later the Captain staggered back in looking as white as a sheet, and asked us if we were all right, as he had almost collapsed on the way up to his room. With the fresh air coming into the office through the open door we too began to feel weak at the knees, and it was then we realised that we had practically been gassed by the charcoal fumes. If Capt. Wilmott had not gone out when he did we would probably have slept in the fumes all night and wakened up dead in the morning!

I met some interesting characters in Pescolanciano, including the Baron, or "Podesta", who often visited Capt. Wilmott and told us a very interesting story about the town. It seems that about 150 or 200 years ago Pescolanciano was world-famous for its pottery industry. At the same time the King of Naples, who was a keen collector of porcelain articles etc., was employing a man who was recognised as the leading light in the pottery industry and held the position of Royal Pottery Merchant or something similar. One day, however, a few specimens of Pescolanciano pottery came into the hands of the king and he pointed out to his "chief potterer" that these specimens were superior to his. So this fellow got a gang of men together and one night he travelled to Pescolanciano and set fire to the pottery factory, and there has never been another one. The Baron also said that antique specimens of Pescolanciano pottery are still to be found in the Louvre and the British Museum.

Towards the end of January the snow cleared away gradually and a spell of warm, sunny days began. After about a week the snow started again, however, and blizzards made the roads impassable. Although during these winter months the front line was static on both sides and neither British nor Germans were very active, many casualties were caused by routine patrols getting lost in the drifts. Many men went out into the snow at night and were never seen again, and attacks by wolves were quite frequent. At this time 78th Div. was being relieved in the line by Polish troops of the 3rd Carpathian Division, newly arrived from the Middle East. We handed over all our stocks of supplies to Polish A.S.C. at Pescolanciano, and on the morning of 5th February we moved to Agnone about 20 miles further on. On the day we moved the snow began again, and as we were billeted in the disused railway station in Agnone we spent most of our time sawing through railway sleepers for firewood, and smashing goods wagons for the same purpose. Agnone was also a very friendly village, the inhabitants of which had never got on well with the Germans, and we were invited into several houses in the evenings. For about the first week we were the only troops in the town, and then a Polish Recce Regt. moved in with their Bren Carriers, Scout Cars and light tanks. One outstanding day in this town was a dinner I was invited to along with Capt. Wilmott and three other fellows at the house of Signor Quarante, the local charcoal and wood king. He was a very influential man in the district, and had a beautifully furnished house. For dinner we had smoked ham and sausage, spaghetti chopped in little triangular shapes known as "Priest's Ears", and salad, followed by cakes, fruit and coffee, and of course "vino bianco" throughout the meal.

On February 17th we handed over a ration dump in Agnone to the Polish A.S.C., and on the morning of the 18th the bulk of the platoon moved out again to rejoin the company and proceed to the new Div. area. I remained behind with Sgt. "Tug" Wilson and "Snakey" Heel to go to our forward dumps at Torrebruna and Carunchia with the Poles and hand over our stocks to them. For the first day we had our meals with the Poles as arranged, but the rations were so horribly cooked that we decided to scrounge some tinned stuff from them and cook for ourselves. In the evenings we could always rely on a plate of spaghetti in one of the Italian houses. On the day after the rest of the Platoon had moved out the blizzard became so severe that the roads became impassable. On the 22nd we managed to get through to the dump at Torrebruna, and brought back our two fellows who had been up there for nearly 4 weeks, living in an Italian house and doing very well for themselves. On the 26th we reached the more distant dump at Carunchia and picked up another two fellows. On the way back we stopped at Castiglione, and after spending a couple of hours with some of our Polish pals drinking vino in their billet we moved off with them back to Agnone. There were seven of us now, and our business with the Poles being finished we were ready to rejoin our unit, but as all other roads out of the town were still impassable we still had another week at Agnone, living in comparative luxury and free from all discipline. The town mayor used to come up every other day or so to see if we were still there, but all the grumbling couldn't shift the snowdrifts and there was nothing for it but to stay where we were. One night we had a bit of a bottle party with several litres of vino and vermouth and some army rum, and a jolly time was had by all. The cyst which I had been in hospital with at Campobasso was developing again behind my left ear, and this night when we were "in our cups" Snakey Heel decided he could cure it for good by walloping my left ear as hard as he could, which he promptly did, and strange to say this crude treatment was a complete success! The matter in the cyst spurted out, and I was never bothered with it again. As this was our last night in Agnone we went round the town about 10 o'clock saying goodbye to our various Italian friends, and by the time we had visited them all we were well oiled. I'm afraid we upset the village barber by forcing him to observe the black-out regulations when he was shaving a customer by candle light. We never found out whether he finished the shave in darkness or lost a customer!

On the 4th of March we moved off again with many regrets in a Polish waggon to try and find our company, with which we had been completely out of touch for nearly three weeks. We covered the familiar route through Pescolanciano, Carpinone and Pesche to Isernia, where to our surprise there were no traces of snow. From here we headed south-west in the general direction of Capua, which we believed to be the Div. Concentration Area. We were in 5th Army country now and encountered multitudes of Americans and French troops in Yankee Uniforms. We wandered all over the place fruitlessly searching for information as to the whereabouts of our unit, till at last we called a halt in a town called Santa Maria, and having found a billet in a partly empty house we settled down for the night. In the morning we contacted 29th Coy. R.A.S.C. where our unit was drawing rations, and were taken ultimately in their ration truck to our new location. Here we were fortunate to be billeted in a farm house, whereas most of the other troops in the district were under canvas. We were particularly lucky in this respect as it was raining almost incessantly. We had very little work to do in this location, with only guards and pickets to prevent it from being a nice rest, and one of my pals and I got to know an Italian family in the nearby village of Ponte Latone, at whose house we spent most of our evenings.

This was only a brief lull before the storm, however, as at this time our infantry were moving into positions at Cassino. About the middle of February, while we had been snowed up at Agnone, the 8th Army had made its "Secret" move from the Adriatic to the West and was relieving the American 5th Army at Cassino. The 5th Army's progress had been halted here ever since November of the previous year, and for almost five months no advance had been made. The town of Cassino itself had been reduced to rubble with incessant shelling and bombing, but on either side of the town there were hills on which the Germans held strategic positions, and the valley between the hills was under constant fire. One attempt to drive the Germans out of their positions and to effect a break-through had already been made by the Americans and New Zealanders, but it had met with no success and severe losses were suffered. It was quite obvious that the 8th Army's move from the Adriatic to the Cassino front was the prelude to another full-scale attack, and it was therefore no surprise to us when the order came for us to move from our "cushy" location at Ponte Latone. On March 14th we left our billet in the farm-house and went under canvas about a mile down the road, where our Coy. H.Q. was camped in a field opposite the farm of a gentleman named Scirocco Giuseppe (This is an example, incidentally, of the way in which people's names are written in Italy, i.e. surname before Christian name).

In the morning we packed up again, offloaded the G.1098 wagon, checked the G.1098 kit, and loaded it up again. This was the farcical procedure which took place prior to every move we made, unless it was too sudden to allow for this waste of time. The "G.1098" was the equipment held by the platoon, such as tarpaulins, weighing machines, an anti-tank gun, two bren guns, butcher's block, office tables etc., which kept the Staff-Sergeant in a constant state of anxiety lest any of the items should go missing. The equipment was therefore checked before we moved from a location, hours being wasted searching for odd rounds of ammunition, tent-pegs, or other articles which had a habit of getting lost. The equipment was listed on Army Form G.1098, and consequently known as the "G.1098 Kit". Anyway, in the afternoon of March 15th we moved off along the Cassino road, known as Route 6, and after getting lost for some time we eventually arrived at our new location about 9 p.m. and slept in our lorries for that night. On the 18th the platoon was mustered early in the morning, and we were told about the task which had been allotted to us. The 11th Infantry Brigade were to be used with the New Zealand Corps to make an attack across the Rapido River at Cassino, and once a bridgehead had been established on the other side we were to cross the river and open a supply point in San Angelo, which was at this time still in German hands. We moved out right away, and proceeded up Route 6 until we pulled in at the location of our Jeep Platoon, a couple of miles beyond Mignano. Here we were well surrounded by other units. On the other side of the road was a battery of American "Long Toms", which fired at intervals throughout the day and night, giving deafening reports and spouting huge tongues of flame. Just in front of them was H.Q., R.A.S.C., while on our side of the road was a hill which the Yankee artillery were using as an O.P. At the foot of this hill was a small cemetery of

Italian soldiers of the Bersaglieri, killed in action. The area was under shellfire nearly all the time, but we were lucky to be located at the foot of a hill, as the shells fell either to our left or on the other side of the hill. During the night, when Jerry apparently brought out his biggest guns, we could hear the "swish-swish-swish" of the shells as they went over our heads, almost spent, and exploded about half a mile behind us. One salvo dropped in our rear Div. H.Q., one night, and gravely wounded a cook, Jim Lewis, who was temporarily on detachment at Rear Div from our Company.

A very amusing thing happened one morning while we were at this location. The R.A.S.C. band from Aldershot was on tour in Italy at this time, and one day they arrived at H.Q., R.A.S.C. to give a concert to the troops in the area. This was the nearest position to the battle front they had ever found themselves in. At 11 o'clock that morning those of us who were not out on details were allowed to go over to the "C.R.A.S.C." location where about 100 fellows had gathered, including some Americans, to listen to the open air band concert, which, incidentally, was very good. The members of the band were the same fellows whom I had seen when the band came to Woolwich in 1942. However, as I have previously mentioned, the C.R.A.S.C. location was about 100 yards in front of the American "Long Toms", which, when the concert began, were silent under their camouflage nets. But at about 11.30 the huge barrels began to rise until they were pointing upwards at an angle of about 50 degrees, and we could see that they were about to fire a salvo. Of course, the band were completely unaware of this, and it's not hard to imagine the sudden confusion which broke out when four tongues of flame simultaneously licked the air, and a second later there was one colossal, deafening report. I can't remember what they were playing, but the conductor turned a complete circle (he didn't drop his baton!), several members of the band sprang to their feet in terror-stricken astonishment, one trombone-player fell off his stool, and the music petered out in a concatenation of meaningless noises! Then they all looked at each other, smiling in rather an embarrassed way, some with obvious relief, and others who had managed to maintain their composure looking with a sort of "What's-all-the-fuss-about" expression on their faces. However, the concert was instantly resumed and thoroughly enjoyed by all.

There were other incidents at this location which were not so funny. One morning a shell burst in the breach of one of the "Long Toms", killing two Americans and injuring three. One afternoon six Focke-Wolf dive bombers, which we seldom saw in the daytime now as we used to in North Africa, came over and "strafed" Route 6 and the surrounding army locations.

Our stay in this location proved to be only of one week's duration, for the attack across the Rapido never came off, and the proposed D.M.A. at San Angelo did not materialise. On March 24th we moved to where the rest of 328 Coy. was, at our last location, and took over the job of bringing up supplies from the railhead at Vairano and then from the new D.I.D. at Presengaro to 57 Coy.'s D.M.A. on Route 6. We also went to the Field Bakery at Sparonesi for bread (a popular detail).

This happy state of affairs lasted for about two weeks. Work was finished by tea-time, and in the evenings there were inter-platoon football matches, A.B.C.A. talks from the officers, and vino-seeking excursions into the nearby village, where French

Moroccan troops were billeted. Of course, guard duty came round every fourth night.

On April 10th I was detailed with one of my pals to take a load of horse-fodder up to a Mule Pack Transport Coy. near Cassino itself. We had to report first to a Forward Admin. Point, staffed by "Q" Branch, 78 Div H.Q., which we found after turning off Route 6 about a mile and a half before Cassino and climbing up a rough, twisting road to a village called San Vittorio, on a hillside facing Monte Cassino, which became famous as "Monastery Hill". From the Fwd. Admin Point we could look straight across at this hill with the monastery on its summit, the monastery which the Germans were using as a fort, and which caused such a great deal of controversy in the Houses of Parliament at home. Dean Inge, from the luxury of his comfortable home in England, stated that it was consecrated ground and condemned the suggestion that it should be bombed. The men in the front line in Italy contested that it was no longer consecrated ground but had become a strongpoint from which the Germans could bombard our troops. Finally the realistic view and common sense of the fighting men prevailed over the idealistic view and complacent dogmatism of the Dean, and Monastery Hill was bombed. It was bombed for twelve solid hours by relays of R.A.F. bombers. The Monastery was reduced to a mass of rubble. But when darkness came down on that day the Germans were still there, firing bursts of tracer bullets from machine guns into the sky, mocking their enemies and jubilant over their survival of the punishing air raids. They had dug-outs 100 feet under the ground.

The Germans were the tenants of the monastery, then, as we looked at it from San Vittorio that day, and it explained the notices which had drawn our attention at intervals along that rough, hillside road, such as "THIS ROAD IS UNDER ENEMY OBSERVATION", or "SLOW: DUST BRINGS SHELLS". To the left of Monastery Hill was Monte Cairo, or "Castle Hill", not so high, but which our troops had recently captured. Through the gap between the two hills was Cassino, or the remains of Cassino, but we couldn't see it on account of the smoke-screen in the valley. This valley had the nickname of "The Inferno", and from where we stood on the hillside looking down at it with its columns of smoke rising up, and an overall haze obscuring the roads and tracks, it looked just as one would visualise Dante's "Inferno". All this time we were under constant shell-fire, and shells whined over our heads in both directions. It amazed me to see the N.C.Os and clerks of "Q" Branch calmly at their work, without even a tin hat to be seen, and despatch riders playing cards or having a shave in the open, completely unflurried, although Jerrie's 88s were bursting on all sides, some near, some far, but all equally liable to burst in the Forward Admin. Point. Here we were provided with a D.R. to guide us to the Pack Transport Coy. He took us back along the dusty road to Route 6, where we turned right and headed for Cassino. Within ten minutes we were inside the smoke-screen. The smoke was generated in big drums dispersed along the roads and in ditches, maintained by Royal Engineers. After another 10 mins. or so of slow travelling we turned off along another rough track, full of pot-holes and shell-holes till we came to a signpost indicating the mule company's location, spread round the remains of a farmhouse. We lost no time in backing the lorry on to a sled where the fodder was to be offloaded by North African muleteers recruited in Tunisia or Algeria. But suddenly we seemed to be in the middle of a mortar bombardment. I think no sound can be as terrifying as the repeated, rushing, whine of the "Sobbing Sisters", or Minnenwerfer, the heavy, multiple mortars so much favoured by the Germans. I ran aimlessly, but fortunately fell right into a slit trench, my pal Steve Quick at my heels. We stayed there for an hour, during which time hundreds of mortars must have dropped all around. Three fell in the Pack Transport location, but caused no casualties. The dispatch rider from "Q" Branch eventually told us it was time we were moving, and, trembling all over, I drove the lorry back to the main road and out of the smoke screen. The D.R. left us when we came to the road up to the forward Admin. Point, and Steve took the wheel. We drove at the fastest possible speed in the gathering darkness and were never more glad to see the company location. We had been on the outskirts of Cassino itself with a 3-ton wagon, an unenviable experience, but it was the last time I was to see Cassino until after it had been captured by the British and was far behind the fighting line.

HOLIDAYS AND HOSPITALS

On April 12th I went on leave for the first time since I had left England 16 months ago. It was only for 72 hours, but it meant a complete break from the never-ending duties and a change from the too-familiar scenery of Route 6. A lorry picked us up, Cpt. Basil Anderson, "Jock" McCulloch and myself, at 9 a.m. We set off with the rest of the divisional R.A.S.C. leave party to the newly-organised leave camp known as "Axeminster". We headed back along Route 6 to Capua, and about 11.30 we reached the outskirts of Naples. We did not go through the city but turned inland and headed south, passing through numerous little towns such as San Vitalia, Sperone, and Avellino, then climbed for several miles. The descent down a winding, hillside road took us through Bellizi, Piano and several other villages to Salerno. Here we turned right on to the "lungomare", or promenade, and went north along the coast road. We were now in what is known as the southern Italian Riviera, and the scenery was easily the finest I saw anywhere in Italy. It was reminiscent of the Sicilian coast road at Brolo, but much more picturesque. On our left we had the really blue waters of the Tyrrhenian Sea, and on our right the steep slopes of green wooded hills, dotted with white villas, and many terraced vineyards. About 3 p.m. we reached the little seaside town of Maiori (re-named "Axeminster" by 78th Div.) and arrived at the Battleaxe Club, our "leave hotel". This was a large building which looked as if it may have been a college in pre-war days, and it was very well fitted out as a rest camp, considering it was probably the first venture of this kind in Italy. In the dormitories we slept on wooden beds and palliasses, and in the dining hall there were tables and Italian waitresses to serve us our meals. There was also a reading room, canteen and proper wash-rooms. Maiori itself was a very nice little town with quite a number of shops and a long promenade lined with trees. There was a lovely beach, but the weather was a bit nippy for swimming and it was deserted except for an assortment of fishing boats and rowing boats which lay there all day and put out to sea at night. As we walked home to our billet at night we could see a long line of fishing boat lights bobbing up and down on the horizon. Maiori had obviously been a holiday resort and depended on its tourist trade for a livelihood. At one end of the promenade there was a café, "The Golden Chopper", with an open-air terrace where we could have "tea and wads" and listen to an Italian 3-piece band. In the evenings we occupied the ground floor rooms, drinking vino and vermouth and singing lustily. There was also a small cinema in the town.

On the 14th we went on an outing to Pompeii, the famous ruined city at the foothills of the great volcano, Vesuvius, or "Vesuvio", to give it its Italian name. For two hours we were shown round the ruins by an English-speaking guide, and it proved to be extremely interesting. Vesuvius is still a smoking volcano, and as there had been a mild eruption during the previous week there was lava dust lying everywhere. Actually Pompeii was not destroyed by Vesuvius but by Somma, the sister mountain, which is now extinct. That was in the year 79 A.D. We saw the Forum, the city gates, and all the usual temples of Apollo, Jupiter, and Mercury, and the goddess Isis. The Stabian Baths were very interesting, but the best preserved and most interesting of all the excavations was the House of the Vettii, which had belonged to two brothers who were wealthy merchants. It was also used as a sort of private hotel for visitors to Pompeii, for in Roman times the place was also a holiday resort and in this house was also the famous brothel. Lady tourists going round the ruins are steered clear of this particular building, but most of the guides carry little booklets of vulgar pictures based on the drawings found on the walls of the brothel, which they sell like hot cakes to male tourists.

Our guide told us an interesting story of how the Pompeii ruins were discovered. On the coast, a couple of miles from Pompeii, is the town of Torre Annunziata, and long ago the people of this town had to go daily to a mountain several miles away to draw water from a spring, as there was no water supply near the town. Then someone hit on the idea of digging sewers from the mountain to the town and thus saving a lot of labour. It was while they were digging these sewers that they came across the ruins of the old city. This was in the 16th Century, but excavations were not begun until the 18th Century.

After the tour round the ruins we had a horse-and-trap ride into the new town of Pompeii, and spent the rest of the day there. It was quite a nice town, but of course full of allied troops, and the biggest nuisance was the amazing amount of beggars and hawkers who pestered the life out of us everywhere we went, even inside the cafés. We went into the cathedral, particularly to see the beautiful altar, which we were told was worth about one million pounds. It was certainly an impressive sight, heavily bejewelled, studded with diamonds and gold; to the enemies and critics of the Roman Catholic Church, however, it serves as an outstanding example of wealth existing within the Church while poverty and hunger abound in the streets, as was the case in Pompeii.

Later on in the evening we went into an open-air café, where a few Italians sat at small tables and two American G.Is. sat by themselves with a bottle of vermouth between them. As there were only two of us, the Yanks called us over and invited us to share their bottle of vermouth. They were artillerymen who had come back for rest after 92 days in the line, apparently, and were out for a good time. We sat with them until two soldiers, one British and one American, came into the café, produced police badges and told us the place was out of bounds to troops, whereupon we left. The two Americans then offered to take us round the shops and buy us anything we fancied for sending home, as they said they knew that our pay was much smaller than theirs. We refused, but it struck me as a good example of the generosity of most of the Americans I came into contact with.

On the following day I met a "Redcap" who was stationed here with a detachment of the 78th Div Provo Coy and whom I had met several times before when he came to collect rations at our supply points. He and one of his mates were going for a trip up the coast that afternoon in a 15cwt truck and offered to take me and my pal with them, and of course we accepted. It was a grand run along the coast road, through Minori and Amalfi, and finishing in Sorrento, a lovely holiday resort made famous by a song, and deservedly so. I found that this was where the real beauty and charm of the Neapolitan area lay, not in Naples itself but in the surrounding villages, seaside towns and lovely countryside. We spent about an hour sauntering round Sorrento, then returned to the leave camp in time for tea. As this was the last night of our brief holiday there was a big party that night in the canteen, senior N.C.Os and O.Rs all joining together in a rowdy sing-song accompanied throughout by endless glasses of vermouth and vino.

About 9 o'clock the following morning we pulled out, passing through Molina and Pompeii again and arriving in Naples about noon. We decided to spend a couple of hours walking round the city, but of course did not have time to get any real enjoyment out of it. We walked along the famous Via Roma and through the Galleria Umberto, then were taken by a couple of small boys up to a house where we had a plate of eggs and chips costing us 90 lire (4/6) each. There was a Fun Fair on in Naples, and the place was crammed with Yanks, many of whom were walking about arm-in-arm with Italian girls. It is not by any means an

Fergus just before heading off to War in 1942.

Fergus in Brodie Park, Paisley, prior to
leaving for North Africa in late 1942.

Fergus, left, in Sicily in 1943.

Fergus, left, at the Sphinx, Giza, July 1944.

Florence, Italy, 1945.

Spitall, Austria, 1945.

Fergus, right, in Spitall, Austria, 1945.

Fergus, centre, relaxing in camp. Austria 1945.

Fergus, centre, in Kotschach, Austria, 1945.

Fergus, back right, in Kotschach, Austria, 1945.

Fergus, left, in Austria, 1945.

Fergus, third left, in Kotschach, Austria, 1945.

Fergus, left, in Kotschach, Austria, 1945.

Fergus with Austrian family. Kotschach, 1945.

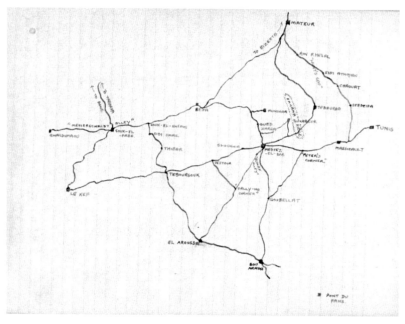

Map of main area of action around Tunis, drawn by Fergus into his diary.

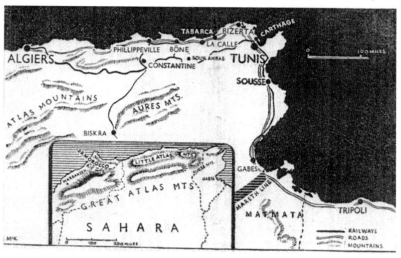

Map showing wider area of action around Tunis,
pasted by Fergus into his diary.

ROMMEL GEFLOHEN!

Feldmarschall Rommel ist mit den besten Leuten seines Stabs nach Italien geflohen ! Das OKW hat die Hoffnung aufgegeben, den Tunesien-Brueckenkopf zu Halten.

Aber Du, Landser, —

DU WIRST IM STICH GELASSEN

Du sollst den Brueckenkopf ohne Bruecke verteidigen, um die Flucht der Offiziere und Spezialisten zu decken. Du wirst ~~nenate~~ ~~damit~~ ~~die~~ ~~Etappenhengste~~ ~~ja~~ ~~Fliegerschutz~~ ~~fuer~~ ~~die~~ ~~Flucht~~ ~~leben~~ ~~koennen.~~ Dir stehen keine schweren Waffen, — denn die sind ja zu kostbar, um fuer Landser verschwendet zu werden.

JETZT KOMMT DEINE LETZTE CHANCE

Eure Transportflugzeuge werden abgeschossen. Eure Transportschiffe werden versenkt !

Du hast nur die Wahl zwischen Tod und Gefangenschaft. Warum sterben fuer eine aussichtslose Sache ? Warum willst Du Dein Leben hergeben, wenn die Staebe sich in Sicherheit bringen ?

BRING AUCH DU DICH IN SICHERHEIT

Fuer Dich gibt es nur einen Ausweg aus Tunisgrad. Es ist der einzige Weg, der Dir Ruhe und Frieden, — und ein Wiedersehen mit Deiner Familie bringt.

FUER DICH GIBT ES NUR EINEN WEG NACH HAUSE : UEBER DIE GEFANGENSCHAFT !

'Rommel Has Fled'. Leaflet dropped to German troops during North Africa campaign.

Front of German propaganda leaflet dropped to British troops in Italy.

Back of German propaganda leaflet dropped to British troops in Italy.

Eighth Army Service of Thanksgiving.

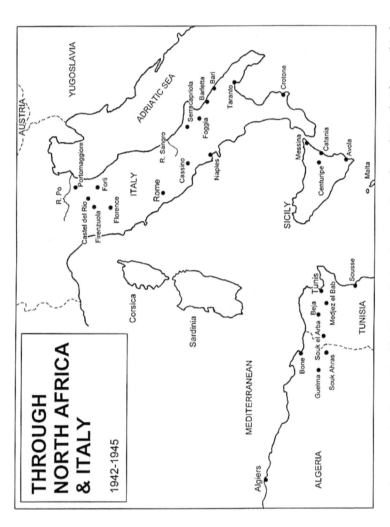

Map showing main places visited by Fergus during the campaigns through North Africa and Italy.

attractive city, in my opinion, and although there are many fine buildings the main streets are narrow and the back streets are filthy. Nevertheless, it is a lively, gay city and I liked it better on my second visit about six weeks later. At 2 o'clock that afternoon we moved off again, and travelled back via Capua to the company location on Route 6.

The next day I went on a detail to Presengaro, my last detail for 328 Div. Troops Coy., and that night I was on guard, my last guard for the said Coy., for while I was doing my two-hour "stag" the Staff-Sergeant, Johnny Mann, came and told me that I was being posted to one of our "sister" companies, the 57th Infantry Brigade Coy, R.A.S.C., and would be joining them in the morning. Their Composite Platoon was under-strength while the 328 Coy. Composite Platoon was over-strength, and to balance things up I was being posted. I was quite pleased with the news, for although I didn't know how my new unit would turn out I was pretty fed up with 328 Coy, which had gained the reputation of being the least efficient of the four Divisional R.A.S.C. companies. Of course, it was a bit of a wrench to have to leave all my pals, but in the Army one learns to expect these things.

My first day in 57 Coy was spent at their Company H.Q., which was a bit further up Route 6, and where I was interviewed by the O.C., Major Seamore, who was also fairly new to the unit. He was a tall, lanky individual who was popularly known as "Longshanks" amongst the O.Rs and was regarded generally as something in the nature of a huge joke. I could see the force of this when he started to relate how in the desert campaign his unit's ration returns were written out on toilet paper, ending his story with a sort of inane chuckling. When the Sergeant-Major, who was standing beside me, broke into loud guffaws I took my cue and also laughed heartily, thus showing the Major that his jokes did not go unappreciated. During my long stay with 57 Coy I was to see many more examples of this remarkable Major's peculiar habits. That night I spent a few very happy hours with the D.Rs in their tent, and the next day I was taken down to the Composite Platoon, who were just north of Capua and were running a D.M.A. (Divisional Maintenance Area). They seemed a decent bunch of fellows, the N.C.Os included, and the Platoon seemed much better organised and more confident in its work than its opposite number in 328 Coy. I was more or less settled down in my new job and getting to know the fellows when I took a dose of malaria, and on April 30th I was taken into 152 M.D.S.

Malaria hits you hardest during the first two or three days, depending on how severe a dose you have, and I lay on a stretcher in a tent at 152 M.D.S. for two days, not caring much whether the war was lost or won, and unable to eat, apart from the periodical doses of quinine. From here I was evacuated by ambulance to 72 General Hospital at Cancello, where we occupied proper spring beds with clean white sheets and were very comfortable indeed. By this time I was beginning to recover and was no longer bothered with high temperatures, but when I got out of bed and stood up I realised how much the fever had weakened me. It was quite an effort to walk the length of the marquee. But it was fine to lie in bed and have your meals brought to you, or talk to the sister who was a Glasgow girl and had done her training at the Royal Infirmary. And then, of course, there was the chap at the top end of the ward who had the gramophone beside his bed and spent the day playing our only two records, Vera Lynn singing "When They Sound the

Last All-Clear" and Bing Crosby singing "Silent Night". On the 4th of May I was taken in an ambulance to Caserta Station and put on an ambulance train. I spent the night on a stretcher in this train, and I was very thankful I was still being treated as a "bed" case, as the poor unfortunates who were now up and about had to sit all night cramped up on the wooden seats in the usual Continental 3rd Class carriage. At 8 p.m. we moved off eastwards, and when I awoke in the morning we were in the station at Barletta. Later on we arrived at Bari, and here another ambulance took me to 98 General Hospital, a fine set of big modern buildings just outside the town.

I spent 10 days here in comfort and ease, well cared for and without a single worry. My ward was a big U-shaped room, bright and airy, and filled with fellows in more or less the same state as myself, with either malaria or jaundice. One or two had bad vomiting spells at certain stages of the quinine treatment, but it never gave me any bother. My sister was an Irish nurse from Inniskilling, and the staff also included Medical Corps orderlies and Italian servant girls. After about 5 days I was allowed to get up and draw a suit of "blues", and was then moved out of the ward into a tent, where, however, our comfort was by no means decreased. In the tents we were looked after by Nigerian orderlies instead of sisters, and before I left the hospital I had a chance to take a real bath, the first real bath I had had since I left England.

On May 15th, my 21st birthday, I was discharged from hospital and went to 197 Transit Camp in Bari. As soon as we had got our kits made up and our beds made down, three of us went off into Bari and spent a very pleasant evening, first at the Toc H canteen and then at the Allied Forces Theatre, where we heard a first-rate piano recital by Capt. Arthur Rubinstein followed by a film called "Destination Tokyo". That night we slept on the stony, bumpy floor of an I.P. Tent, quite a come-down after the wonderful hospital beds, and the following morning I was in a work party erecting a barbed wire fence round the camp's new vehicle park. At dinner time I saw a few of the Jugo-Slav partisans who were based in Bari and joined forces with British Commandos in making raids on German-held islands in the Adriatic. A wilder-looking lot it is difficult to imagine; they were dark-skinned, tough, and ate like wolves, but the fiercest looking members of the Partisan force were the women, who walked around Bari with revolvers and hand-grenades dangling from their belts. That afternoon, after dinner, we went off again into Bari and had another good time, including a visit to the excellently equipped Corner Club for British troops. It was the first big club of that type I had seen in Italy, although N.A.A.F.I. gradually got them organised in every city our troops occupied. About tea-time that day two German planes swooped over the city and flew off again, drawing some Ack-Ack and causing quite a panic among the Italian womenfolk.

On 17th May I found myself in a draft of about 20 men bound for 159 Transit Camp, near Naples, but before going to the railway station we picked up 8 prisoners at a C.M.P. depot, whom we were to escort to Naples. The thing was done in such a haphazard fashion (we were not even armed) that it is not to be wondered at that 5 of them escaped at dusk in a railway junction near Foggia. It was very quickly and easily done. At the end of the carriage was a lavatory and also an open window. One of our party was placed at this window, ostensibly to guard it, while the train was stationary. Two of the prisoners went down on a pretext of using the lavatory, and another three must have left their compartments and hung about in the corridor. As soon as the train started to move, the two at the lavatory pounced on the unfortunate "guard" and held him down while the other three scrambled out of the window. The first two then released the guard and jumped out before he could raise an alarm. We got a glimpse of them through the window of our compartment, running away from the railway track in the gathering darkness, while our train increased its speed and soon left them far behind. The Sergeant in charge of our draft was a bit worried about the incident, but fortunately neither of the two prisoners in my compartment was involved. We had the Military Police-men in the compartment, both ex-hospital cases, who were only members of the draft the same as the rest of us were, but who decided they had better take a note of the incident in their report books. I don't think any of the escorts would hear any more about it.

It was a rotten journey, sitting up in a cramped position all night, and it was a relief when we arrived at the central station in Naples about 6 a.m., where we waited till 4 p.m. before a lorry came to pick us up and take us to 159 Transit Camp. It was a big camp, consisting of both Nissen huts and tents spread out amongst the trees in a vast park, and there was a good NAAFI with a lounge and an orchestra. At noon on the day after our arrival we were granted passes to Naples, and I took the oppor-tunity to go to the San Carlo Opera House where a first-rate company were performing "La Boheme". The theatre itself was magnificent, and the singing was the best I have ever heard. It was here that I saw for the first time how an actor's performance can "stop the show". The principal tenor and soprano were singing the duet "Che Gilida Manina" ("Your Tiny Hand is Frozen"), and when they came to the end of the aria the burst of applause and cheering was terrific. Most of the Italians in the audience were up on their feet shouting "bis", or "encore", and would not be satisfied until the singers had repeated the whole aria again, when after a long burst of applause and more cheering and shouts of "bis" the opera was allowed to proceed. This took place three times during the show. All this took me by surprise the first time I witnessed it, but later on I found that it is quite the customary thing at Italian operas when the performance merits it.

During all this period when I had been reclining in hospitals and transit camps the rest of the army had not been idle. On May 16th a full scale assault had been launched on all fronts (This was the reason why we had been evacuated from the Gen. Hospital at Cancello so quickly. All available space was being cleared for the reception of the expected battle casualties). Cassino had at last fallen to British and Dominion troops, and the Poles had taken Monastery Hill. Wild rumours were flying about, (one to the effect that 78 Division was surrounded and being cut to pieces!) but at any rate it was pretty certain that the forward troops were keeping up the pressure and pushing ahead every day. It was exasperating to fellows like ourselves who had to flounder about from one camp to another in the rear areas while our units were going further and further away from us.

On our second morning at 159 Transit Camp we packed up and moved again, this time to No.1 R.G.T.D. at a place called Nola, about 15 miles from Naples, but no further north. This was a former Italian barracks which had been turned into a training depot for British troops newly arrived from "Blighty", and a sort of "Holding Battalion" for ex-hospital drafts like us. Life in the establishment was pure hell. I spent 8 days here, during which time I did two 24-hour guards, and a 12-hour guard, two route marches, three exhausting sessions on the assault course, and a couple of fatigues. The food was terrible, the discipline sickening, and the parades unending. For our entertainment in our free time (if anyone ever had any) there was a theatre, a library, and a canteen available. However, the one good point about coming to this depot was that I met one of the lads from my own unit, "Nobby" Nobbs, who had also been in hospital, and was now in transit like myself. We shared our sorrows together.

On May 28th we marched off with a sigh of relief to Nola Station and boarded cattle-trucks, which brought us after a 9 hour journey to a goods yard near Vairano, from where we made a 3 mile march to No. 4 C.R.U. This camp was fairly cushy compared to the G.R.T.D., and the 8 days we spent here were quite bearable. Fatigues, which occupied our time in the mornings, were easy, and the afternoons were devoted to baths, medical inspections, etc. Football games took place almost every evening and there were several ENSA shows, film shows, a camp concert, and a performance by the R.A.S.C. Band. One day we saw a tragic air accident. Two Spitfires, almost overhead, seemed to be flying dangerously close, when one of them suddenly started to soar straight upwards in order to avoid a collision. He was too late, however, and his tail cut the other plane in two. Both planes crashed, and we saw the pilot of the first plane bale out, but the pilot of the plane which was cut in half was still at the controls when he hit the ground.

On June 4th we moved from 4 C.R.U. northwards, along the old familiar Route 6 to Cassino, which was an absolute shambles, past the foot of Monastery Hill, and on to a Corps Transit Camp, our last stopping place before rejoining our units. In my tent at this camp there was a fellow who put a razor blade in his mouth, broke it and crunched it with his teeth and swallowed it. To make sure there was no fake about this extraordinary feat I gave him one of my own Gillette blades and he repeated the performance! On the following morning we moved off early, passing through Frosinone, which showed signs of the recent shelling, and about 6 miles further on we arrived at long last at 57 Coy. H.Q. After reporting to Coy. Office we made our way to the Composite Platoon location, where I found a bulky pile of letters and newspapers waiting for me.

ROME: THE BIG PUSH

On June 9th, four days after my return, we once again packed up and the whole Company moved out, northward bound. It was an exasperatingly slow journey, on traffic-jammed roads, through towns which bore marks of the recent fighting, such as Ferentino, Valmontone, and Labico. The sides of the road were littered with burnt-out lorries and tanks, left behind in the German retreat, and we crawled along in the midst of convoys of British and American vehicles. About 8 p.m. we reached the suburbs of Rome. We travelled along several of the wide, main streets, without actually going through the centre of the city, but seeing enough to make us wish we were stopping there. Blocks of big modern buildings, schools and huge hospitals, and a vast sports stadium revived memories of a city life we had almost forgotten. The streets were all lined with trees, the people were all smartly dressed, and the girls were all beautiful. Although we were only passing through a corner of it, it was easily the finest city that any of us had seen since we left England. Later on we were able to spend some more time in Rome, and it is still the finest city I have ever been in. We crossed the River Tiber by the old Pope Pius VII Bridge and were soon regretfully leaving the city behind, although even when we were several miles away we could see the dome of St. Peter's Church. We camped for the night in open fields about 30 miles north of Rome, and on the following morning set off again on another exasperatingly slow journey.

We were on Route 3 now, and when we passed C., R.A.S.C. located at the side of the road we knew we must have reached the Divisional location area. The convoys had thinned out by this time and we were making quite good speed when we suddenly had to drop to a slow crawl again. We were approaching a big diversion which necessitated slow progress, and at the same time we came under shell-fire, the first I had experienced since Cassino. Jerry had left a rearguard of two or three big guns which had selected this diversion as a target, knowing that slow-moving columns of vehicles would be passing through it all day long. It certainly cramped our style a bit, as a policeman had to be posted at the beginning of the diversion to control the traffic, allowing vehicles to set off in groups of five so that there would be no traffic jam right in the middle of the danger spot. For about an hour we were only able to move a few yards every few minutes while intermittent salvoes of shells whined over our heads and dropped about 50 yards away in a field. Fortunately he hadn't quite got the range. At length we reached the start of the diversion, which curved downwards into a sort of hollow and rose steeply again on the other side. The bridge which had spanned this hollow had been blown up by the retreating Germans and the R.Es had therefore been forced to create this rough track down the hillside. With four other lorries in front of us we set off to cover the quarter mile or so of this diversion at the fastest speed possible, which was dead slow in order not to raise dust. We got through without interruption and were well up the other side when the next salvo of shells dropped in the hollow about five yards from the diversion. Once on the main road again, a few minutes driving brought us to the town of Civita Castellana. We went straight through this and eventually arrived at our new location in some woods about 10 miles north of the village. There was a farm here, and in a part of the grounds behind the farm a German unit had built little wooden huts, big enough for three or perhaps four men, in which they had billeted themselves until the recent retreat. They looked much warmer than our bivouacs and I.P. tents, but we were not allowed to enter them for fear of booby traps, so we pitched our tents under the trees and prepared to set up our supply dump.

As the German rearguard was only about 2 miles down the road at this time we were well within shelling range, and although he was concentrating most of his fire on the diversion which we had lately crossed he did send one or two salvoes into the woods in which we were camped and the main road on the left flank. However, apart from the noise the night passed quite uneventfully, and in the morning we had most of the Div. units coming in to draw rations and bringing good news of the infantry's rapid progress. Indeed, the advance was so swift that our supply dump only lasted one day, and one of the other R.A.S.C. Coys "leap-frogged" us and opened another D.M.A.

about 20 miles further on. We remained in this location for another three days and nights, well out of shelling range by now, and having a nice restful time. The only bad point about this camp was that we were pestered by quite a number of big black spiders, which seemed to drop from the trees and wandered in and out of our tents. We called them "Black Widows", but I don't think they were dangerous, and as we were using mosquito nets now we managed to keep them out of our blankets. In Civita Castellana there seemed to be plenty of vino for sale at cheap prices (the inflation which the allied advance always brought with it had not reached here yet) so we brought several "fiascos" of it up to the camp, and we had also acquired about a gallon of "buckshee" army rum (Rum issues usually got slightly out of hand when the division was on the move and we couldn't help being left with a surplus on our hands!). So on our last evening in this location we had a "housey-housey" session (with refreshments throughout) followed by a sing-song and an all-round drinking party. It was the first "social evening" of that type I had taken part in since I left 328 Div Troops Coy, and after I had sung one or two of my "party-pieces" and shown that I could drink along with the rest of them I felt that I was now properly accepted as "one of the boys." 57 Coy Composite Platoon, although they were friendly enough and helpful to newcomers, were slow to accept you as one of themselves, but once they had sized up your character and your nature and found you to be "a good bloke" according to their own standards they became the best pals you could wish to have. They were a grand bunch of boys, and I made many firm friends whom I was sorry to part with when the inevitable time came.

Our three easy days passed all too quickly, and on the evening of 15th June we moved out again. We went north through Ronciglione and Viterbo, and almost 10 miles past the latter we rejoined the rest of 57 Coy. Next morning we were off again and carried on through Castiglione until we came to a farm near a former German H.Q. where we stayed the night. On the 17th we continued our northward route through Orvieto and Ficulle, where we reported to C.R.A.S.C. for orders. We passed through a village called San Lorenzo and were supposed to be going on to the next town where we intended to set up a D.M.A. We were about a mile and a half away from it when we were stopped by an officer from Brigade H.Q. who told us that the Germans were still holding it and we better not go any further. We parked alongside a small cemetery, and as it had been raining all morning most of us trooped into the morgue (there were no corpses in it) and marked out bed-spaces all round the walls. However, Capt. Fowell decided it was consecrated ground and we all had to troop out again. There was no other suitable place in the vicinity for us to camp, so eventually we had to set up our "bivvies" in the wet ground between the tombstones, which were just as consecrated as the morgue in my opinion, and settle down for the damp night. A battery of 25-pounder guns had entrenched themselves about 200 yards up the road and maintained a colossal din all night long. The Jerries seemed to be firing mortars to add to the general noise, but fortunately they were dropping about half a mile away. The following night we were still here, but on the third day we moved off again. We climbed to the top of Panicale, overlooking Lake Trasimeno, and as the infantry had circled the hill on which the town was built we were the first troops to enter the town itself after the

Germans withdrew. The short main street and the village square were deserted, but gradually one or two people emerged from the houses and smiled at us a bit doubtfully. We did not pay much attention to them, however, as the square where our lorries were parked overlooked the wide plains below the town, with Lake Trasimeno on the right, and from our position we could watch the fighting going on not a mile away. We saw two tanks attacking two buildings which were evidently German outposts, and after the tanks had fired several shells at them a white flare was sent up from the nearest building signifying surrender. Shortly afterwards an armoured car of the 56 Recce Regt came up the hill from the plain, and then the Lancashire Fusiliers came out of the line and began trooping into the town. Almost at the same time the Northants battalion arrived on foot from the same direction as we had come and went down the hill to take up positions on the plain facing the German defence line, running east to west on a level with the town of Castiglione del Lago. We could just see the town in the distance on a peninsula which jutted out into the Lake.

The D.M.A. which we were supposed to open in this town never came into being, as all roads leading up to the town were under German observation and it was too dangerous for units to send lorries up to draw rations. During our first night here convoys of lorries arrived with ammunition and we spent the whole night unloading them, but in the morning C.R.A.S.C. must have decided that we were too far forward to function properly, and another R.A.S.C. Coy opened a D.M.A. a mile or two further back. The trouble was that Jerry had evidently decided to make a stand on the plains round Lake Trasimeno and our infantry had not been able to dislodge him from his defence lines as quickly as was expected. Up till this time we had been in front of our own guns, but on our second day here the 25-pounders moved around the hill and installed themselves on the slopes overlooking the plains. On the night of 23rd-24th June we were shelled all night long, but the only building which suffered any serious damage was the one which housed 11 Bde. H.Q. It was here that I first met Cpl. Alex Baikie, who belonged to my unit but was permanently attached to 11 Brigade H.Q. as the Brigade R.A.S.C. Officer's assistant.

On the 24th our guns laid down a great barrage to "soften up" the German positions prior to an attack by our infantry, and, although progress was not so rapid as it had been during the past two weeks, the attack was a success. There were heavy casualties, but the Jerries were pushed out of their line and streams of prisoners came into Panicale. On the 27th we moved out of the town and down into the valley, where we took up a new position in a farm near the main road. Our ammunition dump "opened for business", and it was quite good to start work again after so many days of uncertainty. The people in this farm were the most hard-working Italians I've ever met, and they were very friendly with us, much more so than the people in Panicale. We were kept awake three nights in succession at this place by nuisance raiders bombing and strafing the area. The rest of 57 Coy., who were about 10 miles behind us, were having an open-air film show late one night when one of these raiders dropped anti-personnel bombs all round them and scared them out of their wits.

A rumour arrived one day that the division was coming out of the line and that we were either going home or to Palestine. The "going home" rumour was one that cropped up every now and again and was soon dispelled, but the Palestine rumour was a new one. There was therefore great excitement when it was suddenly announced that our Platoon was to act as an advance party in the forthcoming move and was to proceed south forthwith. It turned out afterwards that Egypt was to be our destination and not Palestine, but it was great to think that after almost two years of constant operational duties we were at last going back for a rest.

On July 4th we packed our kits and loaded the wagons, leaving out only what was necessary for one night's sleep and the following morning's breakfast. That night we finished all our locally purchased vino in a rousing sing-song and bottle-party, and the next morning we moved out to start our 140 mile journey back to the divisional concentration area. We passed through the recently captured towns such as San Lorenzo and Ficulle again in beautiful sunny weather this time, and down Route 2 through Montefiascone. We stopped once for a "brew-up", and at about 3 o'clock reached the suburbs of Rome. We then turned inland and travelled east for about 20 miles to Tivoli, where we camped in an olive grove.

The next morning I was granted a pass into Rome. We set off early in a 3-ton lorry, which we left in the car park at the Ponte Palatino, then Joe Bellamy, Bob MacDonald and I got together and wandered off into the city. We walked past the Temple of the Vestal Virgins and the Campidoglio to the Roman Forum. From here we went via the Arches of Titus and Constantine to the Colosseum, where the Yanks had an information booth and a loud-speaker giving lectures on the history of the Colosseum. From here we walked along Via dell'Impero to the magnificent Victor Emmanuel Monument and Tomb of the Unknown

Soldier, built during Mussolini's time, then round to the Trajan Forum and the Y.M.C.A. Here we got a cab which took us past the Pantheon and over the Ponte Vittorio Emmanuele to St. Peter's Church and the Vatican City. Although the various Roman ruins we had seen during the course of the morning were no doubt of tremendous interest to those who are keen on ancient history, such as my schoolmaster pal Joe Bellamy, I must confess that ruins more or less leave me cold. If there's any sight-seeing to be done I am much happier going round modern (or at least comparatively modern) buildings which are still in use, such as Cathedrals, Art Galleries, etc., rather than the remains of ancient civilisations. For this reason I was far more enthusiastic over St. Peter's Church than over any of the Roman ruins we had seen. St. Peter's is a wonderful place. In front of the church there is a great "Piazza", or "Square", in the centre of which stands a high "Basilica", or column. Inside the church we saw famous paintings by Raphael, many statues and mosaics, and of course the great dome. After having a look through the gates of the Vatican, where Swiss Guards were on constant duty, we took the cab back to the Corso Umberto, and began wandering about again. Having had enough of sight-seeing we went for a few drinks and then to the Teatro Splendore, where we saw a great show by a variety team called the Three Bonos. After this we found a restaurant called the Ristorante Bologna where we had a very satisfying dinner of soup, steak and vegetables with olive oil, fruit and a bottle of Capri Bianco. Next we went to an open-air show in the gardens of the building which had been turned into an E.F.I. Canteen. By the time this finished we were ready for tea, which we had in the Canteen, then walked round the corner to the Piazza Esedra. We could hear dance music coming from one of the buildings, and to our surprise we discovered that a local School of Dancing was running a dance "in honour of the Allied Liberators." It was the first time we had come across a dance of any description since leaving England, so we went in and although none of us got up to dance (we were wearing boots and were footsore with trekking round Rome) we enjoyed listening to the jazz band and watching the others dancing. When we left here we had a walk round a nearby park, which was full of children, fellows and girls, and allied troops, and looked like any Glasgow park in the height of the summer, then gradually made our way along the Via delle Quatro Fontane to the car park. We got back to the camp feeling tired (it was about midnight) but glad that we had at least had the opportunity of spending a day in "The Eternal City".

On the following day we went for a swim in a reservoir near Tivoli, and in the evening we took a walk up into the town itself. It was a stiff climb, and in the town there was nothing of interest except a café where we had some soft drinks. However, there was a fine view of the surrounding countryside, and the long aqueduct which stretched from the high reservoir down to the power-house on the river.

While we were here we handed over our vehicles to an advance party of the 56th (London) Division, who were coming back from a 3-months rest and training period in the Middle East, and on July 7th we moved off again, travelling along the old familiar Route 6 through Valmontone, Frosinane, Cassino and Capua, then inland to Benevento, where we halted for the night. Next day we carried on through Foggia and several small towns till we reached the outskirts of Bari. We camped here, and as soon as we had eaten some dinner we cleared off into town and had an enjoyable evening. The following day was the last lap in the journey and brought us to Taranto. After spending a couple of hours in the town, parked in a street near the Navy House, where we bought the most delicious ice cream I have ever tasted, Captain Fowell came back with our instructions and we drove to a few miles outside the town, where we "de-bussed" in Camp 4 of the Concentration Area. This was a vast, flat, sandy plain, where we erected our tents and set up a supply dump in readiness for the arrival of the rest of the division. From here we were able to go into Taranto almost every night. There was a big, well-organised N.A.A.F.I., and plenty of canteens, vino-bars, cinemas and shows, the particular favourite being an All-Italian variety show, the "Taranto Follies". After the constant movement of the last few weeks it was nice to have a regular daily routine and free time in the evenings. Since I was discharged from the hospital at Bari I had travelled hundreds of miles by train and lorry, and had unrolled my blankets in dozens of different locations, from barracks and Nissen huts to graveyards and olive groves. We were not to remain static for long, however, and on July 17th we moved out while Infantry units of the 56th Division moved in. We marched to Taranto Docks and were packed onto a lighter, which took us out to troopship "Durban Castle". This time bunks were allotted to us instead of hammocks, and we spent our first night in the harbour, watching the lights of Taranto. I think there is no more nostalgic sight than the twinkling lights of a town seen from a ship in the night.

On the 18th, at mid-day, we moved out of the harbour and joined our convoy. Next morning we watched the coast of Calabria slipping over the horizon, and were soon in the open Mediterranean.

4. EGYPT

The voyage to Egypt took five days, during which time nothing exciting happened, and the only features of interest were the usual ones, i.e. over-crowding, stifling heat below decks (which forced us to sleep on deck every night), and, of course, no canteen. On the whole it was a relief to see land again when on the evening of July 22nd we docked at the entrance to the Suez Canal in Port Said. About mid-day on the 23rd, when the sun was at its height, we disembarked, carrying gigantic packs, but fortunately a train was waiting a couple of hundred yards from the dock. As soon as we came off the ship we were besieged by locals trying to sell us anything from diamond rings and watches to obscene postcards. One black-faced, fez-hatted youth grinned at me and said, with a perfect Will Fyffe accent, "Dae ye come from Aberdeen, Jock?" Apparently the pipe band of the Inniskilling Fusiliers, who had played on the mole throughout the disembarkation, led them to believe that we were Highlanders. The train, which was considerably superior to the cattle-truck efforts of past experience, took us across barren country to El Quattara and Ismailia, then on to Quassasin, where we detrained.

From here we were transported in lorries to our camp a few miles away, and were pleased to see that in spite of the semi-desert stretching all around us as far as the horizon the main road had canteens and "cinemas" at intervals of about one mile all the way along.

We were housed in Indian I.P. Tents, 6 men to a tent, and had several marquees as mess-tents, guard room etc. Each man was provided with a bamboo cane bed to keep him off the sand. Unfortunately, scattered here and there amongst the tents were several large, fenced-in, trench latrines, and with the weather as hot as it was the atmosphere in the vicinity of these installations was not of the sweetest.

As it was expected that Composite Platoon would be moving off within a couple of weeks as advance party to a new area, rumoured to be Palestine, we were the first of the Company to be sent on leave to Cairo. On the 26th the whole platoon boarded some big lorries and trailers in the early morning and set off into Tel-el-Kebir on the north road alongside the Sweet Water Canal. There was next to nothing worth looking at on this road, except one village, a prison, and an occasional group of palm trees. About 1 o'clock we arrived in the suburbs of Cairo, and finally de-bussed at Cairo Main Station. There we were allocated to various native guides who were to take us to approved hostels. These hostels, however, all seemed to be full before we got there and when we eventually succeeded in shaking off our guides we got into touch with a respectable-looking Egyptian who took us to a boarding house at 54 Malika Farida Street, which, although it was not one of the approved hostels, suited us very well and went under the name of "Lucky Rest House".

It is impossible to note all the events and experiences that came our way in Cairo in their chronological order, but there are many highlights of this 5-day leave which are unforgettable.

First and foremost is the visit to the Pyramids and Sphinx at Gizeh (or Giza). We went in a party under the auspices of the Y.M.C.A., travelling by taxi. Our taxi-driver nearly killed us all before we were even out of Cairo, but as there was only one window smashed he just laughed carelessly as if it happened every ten minutes. There's a fine motor-road out of Cairo along which we soon covered the 15 odd kilometres to Gizeh, and here our guide took over and we began the tour of inspection. The Pyramids are indeed an impressive sight, and when you have looked at them for a little while you realise what a colossal task it must have been for the ancient engineers and slave-labourers with their primitive equipment. We went into the temple in front of the Pyramid where King Chiops was entombed and by the light of a candle we saw the solid blocks of granite which the tomb is constructed of.

The Sphinx looks just as it does in the photographs, but it was bigger than I had imagined, and I followed the time-honoured custom of having a photograph taken on a horse with Sphinx and Pyramids in the background. The climax of this visit was when we went inside the Chiops Pyramid and in pitch darkness clambered, or rather crawled, up steep and slippery ramps into the centre of the Pyramid. The only guiding light was a flickering candle held by an elderly Egyptian somewhere far in front of us. At last we stumbled sweating into the burial chamber, where our pains were rewarded by having the satisfaction of looking into an empty sarcophagus, of which there are many better specimens in the Glasgow Art Galleries. The scramble down the ramps was swifter, but just as awkward as the ascent. The elderly man was so intent on getting a tip from the leader of our party that he ran off with his candle and left us fumbling about in the dark. When we eventually got out we made a bee-line for the buffet, and after quenching our thirst set off back to Cairo. On the whole, it was a very interesting trip.

We went one afternoon with a "dragoman" on a tour of the native quarter, which was out of bounds to troops. We alighted from our garry in one of the bazaars, made our way through the teeming crowds, and came to the Blue Mosque. One is actually supposed to remove one's footwear before entering a mosque, but if we had left our boots at the door we would never have seen them again, so we had them covered with canvas and went in. Our guide pointed out a very colourful cupola over our heads, but I was more interested in watching a young Moslem boy performing his prostrations before the altar of Mahomet. Scattered about on the floor of the mosque were several men fast asleep. We saw the tombs of some historic king and his daughter, and after refusing offers to have our fortunes told and to buy souvenirs we emerged into the street again.

After this we went into a shop where we saw some young boys making silver bracelets, and in the saleroom we spent about an hour bargaining over two handbags. The shopkeeper asked us to sit down, brought us black coffee, and had his daughter parading up and down with each handbag in turn to show us the effect. Eventually we bought them and left the shop with the blessings of Allah. Just outside the door a young boy whacked me across the back of the legs with a stick, but when I turned round to ask him what he was playing at our guide hustled us off with words of advice as to how to keep healthy in Cairo.

From here we took another garry and drove past the Abdin Palace, residence of King Farouk, to the Museum of Hygiene, which proved quite interesting but is the sort of place which can be found in most big cities. Some of the pictures and models were very cleverly done, and some rather nauseating.

With regard to amusement and entertainment, there was every facility for having a good time in Cairo. First-class cinemas such as the Miami and the Diana were plentiful, showing American and British films with French, Greek and Arabic sub-titles. One night we went to one of the open-air cinemas, the Paradis, I think, where the last performance began at 11 o'clock and ended at 1 a.m. We saw a very good all-Negro musical, "Stormy Weather". Another night at the Ritz Theatre we saw an excellent play, "Escape to Nowhere", performed by an R.A.F. company.

We made a few trips to the fine open-air swimming pools at Heliopolis and the Alamein Club, and spent one afternoon watching a cricket match at the Gezira Sports Club.

I was fortunate because my pal Cpl. Bob MacDonald had spent nearly four years in Egypt prior to joining our unit in Italy, and as most of his time was spent at G.H.Q. Cairo he knew the city well and could take Joe Bellamy and me to the best places while other fellows wasted a lot of time finding them out for themselves. He was mad at having to return to Egypt after volunteering for service in Italy in order to get away from the place. However, while we were here it was announced that the limit for an overseas "tour" had been reduced to 4½ years, and as "Mac" had already completed five years foreign service he qualified to be sent home.

When walking round the streets of Cairo one develops a constant thirst for long, cold drinks, and many times during the hot day did we try to quench it with bottles of Stella beer, straight off the ice, in one or other of Cairo's many bars. For snacks, ice cream and ice drinks, delicious fruit salads and trifles, and sheer comfort, the Victory Club was unmatched. We had lunch once or twice at the Empire Services Club and at the Y.M.C.A., the former being preferable as beer could be obtained there at the rate of two large bottles per man. For dinner in the evenings, however, the Parisianna Restaurant was our favourite haunt (Shades of Parsley Omelette, Roast Chicken, Fried Potatoes, Melons and Grapes, and Coffee!) To make these dinners more interesting, a beggar would invariably stand on the pavement outside the window where our table was placed and do conjuring tricks in the hope of earning an akker or two. After dinner we usually went to either the Carlton or the Bodega Bar and drank iced beer until it was time to go to a show or to one of the many cabarets. Of these, the Washington was the best, with a pretty good floor show, but most of the others, such as the Sweet Melody or the Balalaika, were just dives. Many a soldier has drunk himself insensible in a Cairo cabaret and wakened up in the early hours of the morning in some gutter with his money and his pay book gone.

The Egyptians had no great love for British troops, and although we went about unmolested in the main thoroughfares it was unsafe to venture alone into the quieter streets. It was forbidden to carry arms in Cairo, but a lot of the boys bought leather "coshes" which had a fly-swat at one end and a heavy knob at the other end. We particularly had to watch the many boot-blacks who squatted on the edge of the pavements offering to polish our boots. They would shout "shoe-shine, Johnny?", and if you refused or ignored them there were always half a dozen locals lounging about nearby ready to attack you. Moreover, they always seemed to know the difference between a soldier who was stationed in Cairo and one who was only there on leave as we were. The "residents" were never molested, but we were eternally being pestered with people trying to sell us things in the street at extortionate prices, or offering to be our guides for the day.

Our five happy days in Cairo soon came to an end and on July 31st we sorrowfully boarded the transport once again and returned to Quassasin. Shortly after we came back we took over the divisional supply point, which gave us something to do in the mornings. In the afternoons we could go swimming in the Bitter Lakes about 15 miles away, and in the evenings there were the nearby canteens to go to and Shafto's cinemas, where we could be found almost every night. They were the most comical cinemas I've ever been in: big sheds with rows and rows of wooden benches to accommodate about 800 or 1,000 men, they were packed every night of the week and must have made a mint of money. There were usually two breaks in the film while the reel was being changed, and very often the reels were shown in the wrong order. However, they did a lot to break the monotony of life at Quassasin. I also went to a film show in the garrison cinema at Tel-el-Kebir one night, and it was a vastly superior affair compared to Shafto's.

I had another couple of day passes into Cairo, and although the long journey was a bugbear it was worth it to get away from the camp. The second of these day trips to the city turned out to be quite an exciting one. After having lunch at the Empire Services Club we went to a nearby cinema, the name of which I forget, and saw Errol Flynn and Ann Sheridan in "Edge of Darkness". The cinema was situated in one of the quieter streets, and when we came out we started making our way back to the centre of the city. As we walked along a young local of about my own age came along side of us and asked if we wanted to buy a watch. I told him I already had one and indicated it on my wrist, whereupon he asked me if it was a good one and would I sell it to him. Employing a popular army term I told him to clear off, and then he snatched at my watch and tried to jerk it off my wrist. I kicked him in the leg as hard as I could and he scuttled off shouting back at us. It was only then that we noticed there were no other British troops to be seen in the vicinity, and we quickened our pace. By now we could see ahead of us a "round-about" which we recognised as the Midan Tewfik, where Cairo's main shopping street, Shari Soliman Pasha, began. We were only about 200 yards away from it when coming towards us we saw the same young Egyptian accompanied by one of his pals. When we reached them they turned around and walked one on either side of us, speaking in a mixture of Arabic and English to the effect that they were going to slit our throats. Joe Bellamy pointed towards the Midan Tewfik and said he would call the policeman on points duty if they didn't clear off, whereupon the Egyptian at his side spat on him. At the same instant the one on my side bumped me with his shoulder and made another grab at my watch. I hit him on the shoulder and kicked his shins, and he doubled up bellowing. Joe Bellamy gave his man a hefty push and banged him into another local who was carrying a big square block of ice on his head. The ice dropped on the pavement and broke and its owner gave a shriek of rage and grabbed Joe's local by the throat with both hands. We decided this was a good time to leave the noisy scene and we ran the rest of the way to Midan Tewfik, where we were once more amongst the traffic of Cairo's busy main streets.

That evening we dined again at the Parisianna then went along to the Carlton for a few drinks. When we came out we walked into Soliman Pasha, undecided as to how we should fill in the time until we caught the transport back to Quassasin. Suddenly a little way down the road (it was dark by now) we heard glass being smashed and a lot of shouting. After our experience earlier in the day we weren't too keen to get mixed up in a rough-house, but two fellows from 57 Coy. ran across the street just ahead of us and shouted "Come on! They're going to wreck the – place!" We followed them until we came to a big crowd of troops, probably about a hundred, some of whom were inside one of the cabarets overturning the furniture and smashing bottles, and the rest of whom were outside the door overturning a taxi. After a few minutes the whole mob surged down the street to the "Sweet Melody" and invaded it. Waiters and "hostesses" ran for their lives while the more unfortunate ones were collared by mad Argylls and quickly rendered unconscious. Amongst the mob of troops were infantrymen from the Irish Brigade and the Argylls, a large number of Gunners, a few R.A.S.C. and Engineers, and even two Military Policemen from the Div. Provo Coy! What had happened was this. A large number of 78 Div boys had been enjoying themselves at one of the cabarets, when one of them sitting at a table noticed that a girl dancing with one of his pals had deftly slipped his pay book out the breast pocket of his K.D. Shirt (there was a good market for pay books in Cairo). The chap at the table stood up and bounded on to the dance floor, shouting "She's got your pay book!" The girl immediately made a bee-line for an exit, passing the pay book to a waiter as she ran, but she was too late. Every soldier in the place was on his feet, and the waiter was soon caught and beaten up. Other waiters and chucker-outs who tried to intervene were similarly dealt with, the band were chased out of the hall, their instruments smashed, and practically all the bottles in the bar were broken. The girl who had started it all was caught and along with two of her colleagues was stripped and shoved out into the street. From here the troops moved off down Soliman Pasha and methodically wrecked about 6 more establishments, stopping en route to overturn 14 taxis. We learned later that thousands of pounds worth of damage was caused and had to be paid for by the British Government. Some said it was for this reason that the division was sent straight back to Italy instead of going to Palestine for a month as was the original intention.

The real reason for this outbreak was that the fellows were sick and tired of the constant swindling, thieving, profiteering, and cheating of the locals, and the pay book incident which started the riot was only the spark which was needed to set their tempers on fire. Joe Bellamy and I joined in with them for about three quarters of an hour and then cleared off to the car park while the going was good. About 150 men, all members of 78th Division, were arrested and taken to the local barracks. But during the night an officer of the Military Police arrived at the barracks, claimed he was the 78 Div Provo Marshall, and obtained the release of all the men on the understanding that they would be charged when they returned to their units. The men were never charged, and the officer was never heard of again, even although his supposed signature was held at the barracks. We heard later that the troops who were permanently stationed in Cairo were very pleased about the whole affair, as they were in too risky a position to do that sort of thing much as they would like to. But our "riot" was apparently a trifle compared to the pitched battles which had been fought between the troops and locals in Cairo in the old days when the war in Egypt was still going on. When the Australians and South Africans were there the use of hand grenades and revolvers was not uncommon.

Altogether we spent five weeks at Quassasin. Life here wasn't too bad once you got used to the intense heat, lack of really cold water, and occasional minor sandstorms and whirlwinds. The transport platoons were equipped with a complete new fleet of 3-ton Dodges, the company was brought up to full strength, and there were daily drill parades and "ceremonial" guard-mounting parades. One of our Composite Platoon boys, a spirited youth named Johnny Back, was arrested in Cairo for being in possession of a revolver and ammunition (God knows where he "won" them!) and was sent back to the Company under escort. He was put in the guard-room along with the evidence, to await trial on the following morning, and during that night the ammunition clip disappeared from the table on which it had been lying all day. This caused a bit of a rumpus as nothing could be proved against him if the ammo wasn't produced. None of the men who were on guard that night had seen anybody near it, and the whole unit was confined to camp while kit inspections were carried out in the hope of finding it in someone's possession. But it never turned up and Johnny Back went free. A few days later he was again arrested for stealing a W.D. vehicle, driving recklessly through Ismailia, and assaulting a civilian while under the influence of drink. This time Johnny went to a detention barracks and that was the last we ever saw of him.

On September 7th we packed up and moved down to Quassasin Station, where we boarded a train which took us once again to Port Said. That evening we embarked on the "Capetown

Castle", sister-ship of the "Durban Castle", and lay in the Suez Canal for three days, watching other troopships on their way down to the Red Sea and India. While we were climbing up the shaky gangway on to the ship, loaded as usual from head to foot with kit-bag, blankets, big pack and small pack, tin hat and rifle, one of my pals, Jim Arnold, dropped his rifle into the canal. Within a few seconds a little Egyptian boy dived off the side and brought it up from the bottom. He was well rewarded.

This ship was much the same as the last, except that instead of bunks we slept in hammocks on our mess-decks. While still in port we were allowed to sleep out in the open, but after we sailed this was prohibited and we had to stay in the stifling heat below decks. If you went out on deck after dark every five minutes you would hear a rasping voice coming through the loud-speaker saying "Put out that cigarette!"

On the 10th we glided down past the warehouses etc. and the huge Johnny Walker Sign on the Port Said waterfront, and out into the open sea.

Thus ended our brief period in the Middle East.

5.   ITALY

On the morning of September 15th 1944 we disembarked from the "Capetown Castle" on to a fishing boat and were taken across the harbour of Taranto to one of the wharves. We piled onto lorries which took us through the familiar streets of the town and out to the Divisional concentration area about 8 miles away.

While we were here our amusements consisted of going into Taranto in the evenings, where we went to the same cinemas and theatres as we had visited on our previous stay in this area. There was an extremely good show at the Littorio Theatre which we went to two or three times. In the mornings swimming parties were laid on, but the beach was about 20 miles away and the water was pretty cold.

We spent ten days here, until on the 26th, after a violent rain-storm, we moved out and headed north. We by-passed Bari and travelled through familiar country, passing through villages and towns such as Massafra, Casamassima, Capurso, Giovinazzo, Molfetta, Barletta, Trinitapoli, and Foggia. Finally we harboured for the night outside San Severo. Next day we continued the journey along roads which brought memories of 1943 crowding back to us, as we passed through Campomarino, Termoli, San Salvo, and various other almost-forgotten villages. The green rolling countryside round here was really beautiful in these glorious September days, and it was difficult to visualize the hateful, sodden quagmire it had been when the battle of the Sangro was at its height. This was the Abruzzi at its best, a region of green, undulating hills, peaceful forests, and glittering streams, the happy hunting ground of holiday-making Italians from the big cities. We carried on into country which was new to me, through Castel di Sangro, Fossacessa, San Vito, Chieti, and Pescara, which was a fine modern town. We passed the famous Pescara Dams, which the R.A.F. had successfully bombed, and travelled about 20 miles along the coast road till we came to the former holiday resort of Gillianova. Here we pitched our tents on the beach, while the transport was all parked up on the promenade. It started raining, but nevertheless we had quite a successful evening in the town. I went to a barber's shop and enjoyed the luxury of having someone else shave me, then we paid a visit to a fun fair, had one or two vermouths, and finished with dinner in a restaurant.

On the 28th we set off northwards again and soon came to the city of Ancona, which, although it had been the scene of heavy fighting not many months ago, had some very fine buildings and clean, wide streets. We carried on through Senegallia to Fano, where we turned left and headed inland for several miles till we came to a stop and settled down in a location between the villages of Ponte delli Alberi and Frossombone.

The only unusual thing that happened while we were here was that on October 1st I was granted a day pass to the 8th Army Rest Centre at Senegallia, about 15 miles away. Jock McCulloch went with me and we were all set for a good time, but were sadly disappointed. The N.A.A.F.I. club was not yet properly organised and there was the usual endless queue for "tea and wads". Being a Sunday all the shops in the town were closed, and as the restaurants were out of bounds to troops we had to go the whole day without a meal. There were a lot of Polish troops in the town, and as far as we could see almost every one of them had bought a large packet of soap flakes from the N.A.A.F.I. and hurried through the town with it under his arm. We eventually discovered the reason for this soap mania amongst the boys from Warsaw. It turned out there was a house of ill repute down a narrow street off the square in the centre of the town. It must have been a small establishment as only one man could go in at a time, while the rest stood scattered about the square waiting their turn, each with his packet of soap flakes. At any rate, the damsel who was providing their Sunday afternoon entertainment for them would be sure to have Persil-white undies for many months to come!

We were lucky enough to fall in with three Canadians from the 4th Field Coy, R.C.E., and as they had two bottles of vino with them we passed the afternoon in quite a gay spirit. One of them was a Lance/Corporal, until the other two declared he was only a "goddam rookie" and quickly tore the stripes off his sleeves! However, he maintained he had Indian blood in him and they couldn't take that away from him. We came across a pony and trap standing outside a door, so we all piled in and went for a ride round the block, eventually returning the vehicle to a frantic Italian who wept tears of joy when he saw that both pony and trap were still all in one piece and none the worse of the experience.

In the evening we saw a film show at the N.A.A.F.I. and then went back to camp, starving and footsore.

On the following day the rain came down in torrents, and about mid-day word came in that we were to pack up and stand by to move. About 9 p.m., in pitch darkness and soaking wet, we pulled out of the waterlogged location and commenced our move to the central front. The first stage of the journey took us to Ancona and then we turned inland again. The overland road was a veritable switchback, climbing and dropping along the sides of huge mountains, sometimes scarcely allowing room for the lorry to proceed without going over the side, frequently riddled with bomb-craters and always mud-sodden and slippery. It was a nightmare journey, in complete blackness and without lights, but in the early morning the weather cleared and the sun was shining when we reached Assisi. The town, famous for its associations with St. Francis, is built on a hill, and its most outstanding feature is a great Franciscan Monastery. We did not enter the town but came to a halt on the main road and had some breakfast. There was an atmosphere of peace over Assisi and the lovely surrounding country, bathed in the early morning sunshine, and it was annoying to have to climb into the trucks again and move off. During another full day's journey we passed by the northern shores of Lake Trasimeno and the outskirts of Perugia. We halted for the night in a railway station, and on the following day at one o'clock we moved off again northwards. A 30 mile run brought us through Borgo San Lorenzo to the town of Scarperia, where we set up our location.

THE LAST WINTER

On our first night in Scarperia we slept in our "bivvies", but the sudden change of weather, which brought torrential rain, did us a good turn and we were allowed to go into billets. Five of us slept in the front room of an empty house, and the rest of the Platoon in some rooms adjoining the empty town hall. We set up 719 D.M.A. with a ration point in a small park in the middle of the town and a petrol dump spread out along a rough road leading out of the town. An ammunition dump was opened at a village called Sassaleone about 20 miles further on and right on the edge of the battle area.

The divisional Infantry battalions had taken up positions in the mountains south of the Bologna-Imola-Faenza district, and during the next four months a static front was held, with Monte Grande, the highest mountain in the area, becoming one of the bloodiest battle grounds which the war in Italy produced. Scarperia is situated on the main road from Florence to Bologna, and for four weeks we lived a life of comparative ease here, working hard for about twelve hours a day but nevertheless enjoying the comfort of our billets, 20 miles behind the line. But we didn't know what was ahead of us, and before the winter was over I had my full share of the appalling conditions that existed in the forward area.

During the time that our D.M.A. operated in Scarperia the other units in the division, nearly all of which were further forward, had to make a 20-mile run over a tortuous mountain pass, uplift their rations and petrol, and make the same journey back again. American transport was also using this road, which was already in bad condition, and the heavy traffic was not helping to improve it. As the winter weather grew worse it was obvious that a new D.M.A. would have to be opened somewhere on the other side of the mountain pass, and at the beginning of November 720 D.M.A. was set up by 237 Coy. R.A.S.C. in a place called Firenzuola, the first town on the other side of the mountain. In easy stages all the units which had been drawing supplies from our D.M.A. were gradually switched to the new D.M.A., and after about two weeks we closed down. As the working hours decreased we had more time for social life, and I made friends with an Italian family who invited me and another Glasgow man, Tom Harbison, to spend our free evenings in their house. There was always a bit of vino to be had, and I learned several popular Italian songs, the favourite being "Mama" (immensely popular amongst Italian soldiers), "Santa Lucia", and of course "Lili Marlene". One night in our billet we were joined by an American infantryman, Bill Leisner, who stayed with us till the following morning. He was a "litter-bearer", the Yankee equivalent of a stretcher-bearer, and was on his way back from the front line looking for his unit, or so he said. Seemingly he had spent three days crouching in a fox-hole, and when he eventually plucked up enough courage to come out he found that his division, the 85th, had been relieved by the 88th and had gone out of the line leaving him behind. Maybe he was genuinely trying to find his unit or maybe he was just a deserter, but at any rate his jokes and stories and his Yankee humour were priceless.

Shortly after 237 Coy's Composite Platoon had opened the new D.M.A. and got it going it was decided that we were to take over their job, and on November 14th we moved off on the 20-mile journey over the mountain pass to Firenzuola. There was some fine mountain scenery in this short run, but the state of the road was so bad and the precipitous drops so close to the wheels of the truck that we weren't able to fully appreciate the beauty of the countryside. Firenzuola itself, although at one time a fairly big town, was by now a heap of rubble, as it had previously been a German H.Q. and had received the close attention of the R.A.F. There were one or two buildings which were partly preserved amongst the ruins and these we took over as billets. Six of us occupied the top flat of a rickety three-storey house, and by spreading tarpaulin sheets over the leaky roof and draping bivouacs over the windows, and building a fireplace, we were able to make ourselves fairly comfortable.

The mud in this place was the worst I have ever encountered. Every day lorries got bogged down and had to be towed out. On more than one occasion in the dark I would find myself sinking up to my knees in what seemed to be fairly shallow mud. The rain was almost incessant and there was little or no drainage amongst the ruins. On the last day of our stay in Firenzuola it became necessary for men wearing thigh-boots to carry other men across certain parts of the "road" in front of our billet. The terrific amount of work involved in this D.M.A., which kept us at it from 7.30 in the morning till 9.30 or 10 at night, combined with the frequency of the guards and the living conditions, made our three weeks at Firenzuola a rather gloomy period. However, we had acquired an old wireless set in Scarperia and at night we used to listen to excellent programmes from the American Forces Network. Many a night did Frank Sinatra and Glenn Miller keep us awake till one o'clock.

On 7th December we were relieved by 237 Coy, who had had three weeks rest, and we thankfully moved back to a small town, San Piero a Sieve, between Scarperia and Borgo San Lorenzo. On our arrival here we learned of a typical example of the injustice which exists in the army. Before the bulk of our platoon left Firenzuola an advance party had been sent on to San Piero, to prepare our billets. The whole company was stationed in the town, and we were to be billeted in private houses. The advance party consisted of four privates and a L/Cpl, Bill Williams, a very efficient and extremely likeable chap. On their second day in San Piero one of the privates, a despatch rider by the name of George Comber, skipped off to Florence and didn't come back. Bill Williams allowed him 48 hours and then reported his absence to a Sergeant. The Sergeant kept quiet for another 24 hours and then reported the matter to Sergeant-Major Danny Dance. The Sgt/Major didn't report it to anyone. After four days the Military Police in Florence picked up our George in a state of drunkenness and brought him back to the Coy. The O.C. was furious because the matter had never been reported to him and decided that whoever was at fault would have to be punished. The Sgt/Major and the Sgt. decided that they didn't want to lose their stripes so they charged Bill Williams with failure to do his duty. It was only his word against theirs so Bill was reduced to the ranks. If ever there was a flagrant example of victimisation, that was it. However, our own Platoon Officer had different ideas about Bill and a few weeks later he was re-mustered as a Storeman and made up to L.Cpl. again.

In San Piero I was billeted in a room in a civvie house at No.1 Via Medici and things looked quite pleasant, but our "rest period" proved to be short-lived, for on December 9th, two days after our arrival, I was sent off again with nine other fellows to take over a reserve ration and petrol dump at Castel del Rio, a town about 15 miles beyond Firenzuola.

We arrived at Castel del Rio after dark, and for one night shared a billet with the fellows whom we were relieving. On the following morning these fellows moved out and we were able to spread out our kits and make ourselves comfortable. Our "billet" was a former cow-shed with stone floors and a feeding-trough running the length of one wall. On the opposite wall a brick fireplace had been built, and there was a door at each end, one leading to the back yards of the houses in Castel's only street, and the other leading into a field which sloped for about 200 yards down to a river. The shed was about 20 ft. in length by 10 in width, and as there were five of us billeted here we had plenty of room for our beds. I had acquired a door from a bomb-damaged house in Scarperia which I carted around with me and which made an excellent bed, provided we did not have to use bivouacs. Soon after our arrival in Castel it started to snow, and as there was practically no work to do here we spent most of our time chopping wood for the fire and making tea. Capt. Fowell and Sgt. Thomas, who were in charge of the party and the reserve ration dump, occupied a room on the ground floor of the house behind which our shed was situated, and the rest of our personnel were quartered in two other billets in the town. The 217 Field Ambulance Coy were stationed here and had taken over the biggest building in the village as an M.D.S. Rear Div. H.Q. were also here, and the "Castle" at the north end of the main street, which gave the village its name, Castel del Rio or "Castle of the River", was being used as a billet for the infantry battalions as they each came out of the line in turn for a rest. This castle was by way of being a godsend to all of us, for although Jerrie's 88s were sending over shells all day long from about 5 miles up the valley to the north, they all stotted off the thick walls of the castle and never proved to be so much as a nuisance to us. That is, all excepting one momentous night when the Hun decided to give us a surprise.

The first indication we had of the bombardment we were in for was when we heard a terrific bang, louder than any of the neighbouring guns would have made, just outside our billet. We opened the door and looked out, still wondering what was up, when we heard a "swish" above our heads and some slates falling from the rooftops.

This one did not explode, but we knew it was a shell all right. Most of us were in a state of semi-undress, so we grabbed our greatcoats and tunics and ran out of the cowshed into the basement of the adjoining building. As I was running through the passage which led from the back yard to the cellars one of my sandshoes flew off my foot and I stopped to look for it. The rest of the fellows passed me and dived into the cellar at the end of the passage, and as it was pitch dark I gave up trying to find it and hurried on after them. We had no sooner got into the cellar and started putting on our tunics when another shell burst in the passage we had just come through, badly injuring two men not more than two yards from where we stood. The wall of our cellar protected us from the blast, but the smoke and the smell of cordite set us coughing and choking for several minutes. We carried the two wounded boys to the furthest away corner of the spacious cellar and made them as comfortable as we could. They were both unconscious and had wounds in the head, shoulders, and ribs, but were not bleeding much. One of the fellows went off to the M.D.S. for stretcher-bearers, and at the same time Capt. Fowell and Sgt. Bill Thomas came running down the stairs from their room, which was directly above the cellars. This amazing shell had gone through the shutters of the window of their room, through the floor in between their two beds and into the cellar next to ours. It glanced off a beam, broke through the wall of the cellar, and exploded in the passage about three yards away from us. Shrapnel which came flying through the open doorway hit the two fellows who were now lying in the corner, but we were lucky to get off so lightly.

By this time shells were bursting all over the town and we learned later that Jerry was using 240mm guns with super-charged shells, which he was firing from Imola, a town about 15 miles away and he certainly was hitting his target. The main street was packed from end to end with lorries, many of which were loaded with ammunition and petrol and the ultimate losses in wrecked and burnt-out vehicles were 21 lorries and 11 Jeeps. Casualties amongst the troops, however, were only two killed and nine injured. After a while, an order was passed round the cellars for all men who were able to drive to go up into the street and help to move the vehicles out of the town and when we went up the scene in the street was absolutely chaotic. Men were standing on lorries trying to beat out the flames, documents were being salvaged from Rear Div. H.Q.'s burning building and undamaged lorries were trying to worm their way slowly through the inferno. At the end of the street an officer was standing, calm and unflurried, directing traffic round the S-bend which led out of the town. The shells were coming over in salvoes of twenty at a time, with an interval of about half-an hour between each salvo. In four hours, he dropped about 150 shells, including quite a number of duds. Sid Crane and I took his 3-tonner out of the town at about one o'clock in the morning and the bombardment stopped at about two, when we walked back in and slept the rest of the night in a cellar. It wasn't until the morning that I noticed that some small fragments of grit had punctured my right trouser leg and embedded themselves just above my knee but they were easily removed and the scratches soon healed up.

Every day at Castel we had a visit from some young girls who came with laundry for troops in the town and we became very friendly with them. They had evacuated their house in the village and were living in a farm on the hillside across the river, about 2 kilometres away. We eventually became regular visitors at their "house" every night, although the whole family lived in a barn, along with two cows, four sheep and no fireplace. They were such nice people that when in their company we forgot about the discomforts of the place and, despite the bitter cold outside, it was usually fairly warm in the barn.

One day when the girls brought us our washing, the youngest, Matilde, cut an artery in the palm of her hand. The orderlies in the nearby M.I. room bandaged it up and the girls went home as usual but in the evening when we went up to see them we found that she was still bleeding. After a while she lost consciousness and we could see that she had suffered such serious loss of blood that unless something was done soon her life would be in danger. One of the boys went back to the village, got hold of Capt. Fowell's jeep and drove it up the bumpy, winding track to the farm. We wrapped her in blankets and put her in the back, then drove her slowly down to the village again, where the M.D.S. stitched her hand and sent her to a civvy hospital in Florence the following day. From then on, the whole family regarded us as heroes! The sequel to the story took place about ten days later, on New Year's Day, when three of us had a day pass into Florence. We went to two hospitals where we thought she might be and had a most entertaining afternoon walking round the women's wards trying to spot her. Eventually we found that she had been discharged and was staying at her married sister's house in Via Cimabue, where we called to see her and found her feeling fine and enjoying herself.

We spent Xmas Eve in a very happy way at the family's barn, and on Xmas Day we had a slap-up dinner with the 217 Field Ambulance in the M.D.S. Xmas Day and Boxing Day were both occasions for a great deal of drinking and general enjoyment. As an army order had recently been issued that troops could wear khaki ties when off duty we had each had a tie made out of old shirt material and wore them for the first time on Xmas Day, feeling very elegant.

However, on Dec. 27th we reluctantly had to say good-bye to our friends, and on the following morning another party from our platoon arrived to relieve us and we returned to San Piero.

This time I was billeted with four other fellows in a house at No.5 Via Medici, where our hosts were a very nice family who could never do enough for us. They kept a big fire blazing in the living room all day and insisted on us sitting round it with them instead of keeping to our own room. On Saturday nights we dined with the family, doing our best to consume huge plates of spaghetti, and repaying them with occasional tins of bully and bars of chocolate. On Hogmanay we bought some vermouth and Marsala and had a grand time with singing and dancing, bringing in the New Year in traditional style. Wilfie Moore gained unchallenged success as a comedian by suddenly letting his top set of false teeth protrude from his mouth and scaring the children and young girls out of their wits!

But once again the comforts of life in San Piero were only available to me for a very brief spell, for on January 2nd, 1945, I was told to pack my kit and board a 15-cwt truck, which was to take me to the 78th Div Jeep Platoon. As this meant a journey which would last all day and a destination well forward in the battle area I was not very pleased, but orders are orders. I was to relieve a L/Cpl who was going on local leave, and the duration of my stay in the Jeep Platoon was supposed to be eight days, but of course it turned out to be over three weeks. By dinnertime we had reached Castel del Rio, where we stopped for about an hour, and then went on up the valley to Sassaleone, where the Forward Ammunition Point was situated. After a short halt here we moved on along a rough, muddy road which led to the village of San Clemente. About half a mile short of the village we turned off to the right and went along a track to the Jeep Platoon location, which was just at the beginning of the smoke screen which shrouded the forward defence lines.

The Jeep Platoon was made up of about 60 Jeeps and Trailers, whose job it was to deliver ammunition, rations and various stores direct to the infantry in their positions, or to mule transport loading points when the infantry positions were inaccessible by vehicles. Our sleeping quarters were shallow dug-outs covered by bivouacs, which for me was a considerable change for the worse after our homely cow-shed at Castel del Rio. The biggest bugbear was the snow, which often fell to a depth of 8 or 10 inches in a few hours, and the weight of it would frequently cause the poles of the bivouacs to snap during the night. Even when the poles managed to stand up to the strain the tents became so heavily snowed up that their sides were forced right in, and we would wake up with our heads and bodies jammed under the dead weight. It became one of the duties of the guard to rouse us in the event of a heavy snowfall so that we could get out and shovel the snow off the sides. When we got up in the mornings it was usually still pretty dark, so that we were not allowed to light fires and it meant washing and shaving in ice-cold water.

We were surrounded by guns of all calibres, British and American, and there was steady shelling by both sides all day and all night. Although we could hear Jerry's "Sobbing Sisters" dropping in the hills all around us his mortars apparently couldn't reach us down in the valley, but his 88s certainly could and did. About three quarters of a mile up the Jeep track to Ripiano there was a ford across the river which was under fire from a German machine gun. It was a hell of a spot, and a favourite place for Jeeps to break down in the middle of the river.

Another thing which didn't help to make life with the Jeeps any pleasanter was that our officer was Capt. Michael Beer, who had been my section officer two years ago when we were sailing to Africa in the "Llangibby Castle". He was still a useless type and had also proved himself to be a coward. He had been in command of a platoon in a Field Ambulance unit for some time, until one night he was leading a convoy of ambulances to pick up casualties in the forward area. When they came under a bit of shell-fire he turned his car round and cleared off, leaving the ambulances to carry on by themselves. As the drivers had no maps or directions they got lost and suffered heavy casualties in men and vehicles. After that Capt. Beer was posted to 57 Coy., who sent him to the Jeep Platoon.

Life with the Jeep Platoon followed a pretty regular routine, during the day at least. In the mornings the first job was shovelling snow off the Jeeps and trailers, then running the engines for half an hour or so. The rest of the morning could be devoted to maintenance and repairs, cleaning the mud off your kit and drying your blankets if possible. Both my pairs of boots were absolutely sodden, and I ruined one of them by placing them in front of a fire for several hours, with the result that the leather cracked and I had to pay for a new pair. In the afternoons some of the Jeeps went back to Sassaleone and other places to load up with ammunition and other supplies. The real work began at dusk when the convoy set off up the track to Ripiano, delivered its loads, and usually arrived back at the location about 2 o'clock in the morning. What with the bitter cold, slushy, cratered roads, and perpetual shelling it was a nerve-wracking job, but of course we weren't out every night. One evening when I was free I decided to take a trip back to Castel del Rio where the divisional theatrical company was performing its panto-mime "Cinderella". Some of the other fellows had already gone, but I had been out on detail in the afternoon and was late in setting off. I walked down to the main road, such as it was, and thumbed a 3-tonner which was going my way. He stopped and I climbed into the back, which was empty except for what seemed to be several rolls of blankets lying on the floorboards. I didn't pay much attention to them at first, but after a while one of the "bundles" roused my curiosity because of its rather curious shape. I stared at it and looked at the others, and it became obvious the blankets were merely covers for something else. I touched one of them, and it dawned upon me that I was travel-ling in the company of ten dead bodies. The lorry belonged to the Div. Burial Unit.

One day a sensation was created when for the first time in the history of the Jeep Platoon we had a visit from the O.C. of 57 Coy, Major "Longshanks" Seamore. He decided to leave his haven of peace at San Piero and come up to the front for a day to visit the ammo dump at Sassaleone and the Jeep Platoon, who were under command of 57 Coy although the drivers were drawn from all four divisional R.A.S.C. Coys. An amusing story was told later of a dialogue which took place between "Longshanks" and one of the boys at Sassaleone dump. The scene is a mud-soaked bivouac and the dialogue is more or less as follows:-

LONGSHANKS: Good morning. How are you getting on?

DRIVER X: Good morning, sir. Not too bad, sir.

LONGSHANKS: What's your name?

DRIVER X: ----, Sir. "A" Platoon, sir.

LONGSHANKS: Ah, yes. Grub all right?

DRIVER X: Yes, sir.

LONGSHANKS: Had any leave lately?

DRIVER X: Not yet, sir.

LONGSHANKS: Get your NAAFI every week, laddie?

DRIVER X: Yes, sir.

LONGSHANKS: Enough cigarettes, chocolate, etc. ?

DRIVER X: Yes, sir.

LONGSHANKS: Razor blades?

DRIVER X: Yes, sir.

LONGSHANKS: Then why the hell haven't you shaved this morning!!

When he arrived at the Jeep Platoon the Major thought he would like to go for a run up the track to Ripiano, but as he wanted to get back to San Piero that night he wouldn't wait to accompany the convoy at dusk and ordered a Jeep to take himself, Capt. Beer and a sergeant up the track in the afternoon. When they were about half way there they passed two men dressed from head to foot in white snow-suits, which infantry patrols were using at that time. The Major remarked that in these outfits you couldn't possibly tell whether they were British or Germans. Strangely enough, on the following morning the same two men were brought into the Jeep Platoon location escorted by three Military Policemen. They <u>were</u> Germans.

Another very amusing incident took place while I was with the Jeep Platoon, although it was not regarded as being very funny by the authorities at Coy. H.Q. There were three sergeants attached to the Platoon, fine, hearty fellows all of them, and each night it was the duty of one sergeant to go with the Jeep convoy on its detail up the Ripiano track. One night, however, all three sergeants decided to go together, and everyone said they were real decent, fearless chaps, but of course a little bit crazy. So when the Jeep train set off that night the three sergeants rode out in the last Jeep, muffled up in greatcoats, scarfs and tin hats, and pulling a full load of blankets in the trailer. A battalion was moving into the line and we were carrying their stores, G. 1098 equipment, and surplus kit, etc. As we climbed the muddy track in the darkness we were flanked on either side by long single files of slow-moving infantry making their way up to Ripiano. Everything was going well and we looked like having a steady, uneventful night, when suddenly about half-way to Ripiano the three sergeants suffered an unfortunate mishap. The tow-bar with which they were pulling their trailer snapped, and the trailer sank back into the mud with its load of blankets. The sergeants quickly decided that the only thing to do was to go back to the Platoon location, get another Jeep with serviceable towing gear, and resume the journey to Ripiano. Now, the track was so narrow that it was impossible to turn a vehicle round, so in order to go back to the location the sergeants had to carry on up to Ripiano, turn round at the top of the track, and come back down again. When they reached the derelict trailer, they noticed to their dismay that about half the load of blankets had disappeared, and their suspicions were directed against the silent lines of infantry who were still slogging up the track. However, they hurried on back to the location, got hold of another Jeep, and hurried back up the track again. When they drew level with the trailer for the second time they were astonished to find that almost all the blankets were gone and that one wheel had been removed and taken away. It was now absolutely useless to try and get the trailer with the remains of its load up to Ripiano, so the only thing to do was go back to the location again and get a spare wheel. Once more they sallied up to Ripiano, turned round and hurried back down. When they reached the trailer for the third time their curses were long and loud, for the last of the blankets and the other wheel were gone, presumably carried off by members of the Lancashire Fusiliers. When the rest of the Jeeps returned to the location in the small hours of the morning, it was three very sheepish-looking sergeants who reported to Capt. Beer that their night's work had resulted in the loss of a load of blankets, two wheels, and a broken tow-bar. Only then did it occur to them that all the disgrace could have been avoided if one sergeant had been left to stand by the trailer while the other two went back to the location for another Jeep!

My last day with the Jeep Platoon was the worst I had experienced during my period of duty with them, for the best part of the morning and afternoon was spent jumping in and out of the slit trenches. I don't know whether "Fritz" was aware of it or not, but his 88s got the exact range of our location and "stonked" us intermittently for six hours. Then in the evening a German dive-bomber cruised down the valley from the direction of Castel del

Rio, flying at a leisurely pace only a few hundred feet up, and although he was so low that we could plainly see the black crosses on his wings not a single Ack-Ack shot was fired at him until he was miles away from us.

On Jany. 26th the O.C.'s Humber arrived, bringing a L/Cpl. to relieve me and Lieut. Steve King to relieve Capt. Beer. I was in a pretty happy frame of mind, therefore, when as soon as dinner was over I started off in the company of Capt. Beer on the journey back to San Piero. At this time the American 88th Division was moving back into the line after a rest, and I had an amusing episode with a G.I. during the course of the journey. We had stopped at Sassaleone to scrounge a tin of corn beef from the cook at the ammunition dump, and I got talking to a Yankee truck-driver who had stopped for a few minutes on his way up to San Clemente. During the course of the conversation he asked me if Jerry was doing much shelling in this sector, and I casually said that he wasn't giving us much bother, as he didn't appear to have very many big guns. I had no sooner got the words out of my mouth than we heard the ominous "swish-swish-swish" of a salvo of shells passing just over our heads. We flung ourselves headlong into the ditch, and as three shells exploded in the field about 200 yards away the American, with typical Yankee humour, shouted "Well, maybe he's got no 88s, but that ain't hay he's throwin'."

In San Piero I took up residence again at No. 5 Via Medici, and on the following day I had ample reward for my trying period with the Jeeps when I was told that I was selected for seven days leave in Florence.

FLORENCE & FORLI

My leave lasted from Jan. 28th to Feb. 4th, and every minute of it was enjoyable. One of my pals, Arthur Taylor, went on leave with me, and we reported at 54 Rest Camp, a couple of kilometres outside Florence. The place had been a former Italian barracks, similar to the G.R.T.D. at Nola, and all the buildings were being used as either dormitories, canteens, lounges, etc., while there was also a cinema, theatre, church, barber shop, and reading room in the camp. It was possible for one to have a very comfortable leave without moving out of the camp, but needless to say we were never in camp after breakfast, which finished at 09.30 hours, and we never came back till about 10 o'clock at night. Although it was only the beginning of February the short Italian winter was already drawing to a close, and we had seven lovely, sunny days in which to knock about Florence. We spent quite a lot of time at the Robertson Club, the best NAAFI club of its kind I had ever been in up to then, where there was every facility, including a restaurant, snack bars, cinema, games rooms, reading rooms, Italian lessons, W.V.S. "Say It With Flowers" Service, photographer, and three orchestras.

When we were not at the Robertson Club we were either sight-seeing or at one of the many cinemas and theatres. We saw several good films and stage shows, both by ENSA and Italian companies, but one thing by itself which made this leave worthwhile was the opportunity I had to go and see Italian opera performed by a first-rate opera company. At the Teatro Verdi I saw "Tosca" and "Madame Butterfly", both by Puccini, and both magnificently performed. I had already seen " La Boheme" in Naples but I went to see it here again on the last day of our leave, and it still remains my favourite among the operas.

Florence is famous as a city of art, set among quiet hills with soft outlines and gentle slopes, against which the distant Appenines rise more steeply. "Firenze" (to give it its Italian name), capital of the province of the same name, is a bridge town built where the River Arno leaves the Appenines to enter the plain of Tuscany. Europe's Middle Ages ended with a re-birth of art and letters, the Renaissance, centering in Florence, and the height of the city's splendour was reached in the days of Lorenzo de Medici, still known as "Il Magnifico" to Florentines. The Medici were a family of wealthy merchants who lived in the 15th Century and became absolute rulers of the city until they were eventually driven out. To-day, although recognised for its modern straw-plaiting industry and also for its jewellery, porcelain, and glass, it is as a treasure house of Italian art that Florence is universally known. Although the centre of the city was crowded with allied troops of all nations and military transport of all descriptions, and the normal life of the civilian population was completely upset, the character of the city still seemed to be austerely mediaeval. Even strictly commercial buildings in Florence are often architectural gems. The most impressive edifice is Il Duomo, the Cathedral of Santa Maria del Fiore, situated in the Piazza del Duomo, Ruskin's "history-haunted square". Many fine paintings and sculptures of the 14th-16th Centuries, which are normally housed in the Cathedral, had been removed elsewhere for safety during the war, so that there was little left to see inside except the fine dome, finished in 1461 by Brunelleschi. We climbed to the top of the Campanile, or bell-tower, from where we had a grand panoramic view of the city. Also in the Piazza del Duomo is the famous Battistero, or Baptistry, built in the 11th Century, and bordered by stone mosaic pavements dating back to perhaps the First Century. It has recently been discovered that the doors of the Battistero, which have always been taken to be made of bronze, are in actual fact solid gold.

In the Santa Croce Church we saw some beautiful paintings, including the centuries-old original painting of St. Francis of Assisi by Giotto, and the painting of St. Lawrence under torture by Donatello. The church is also known for its remarkable sculptured tombs, including those of Michaelangelo and Galileo. When we were leaving the church the priest who had been showing us round asked us if we would like to leave an offering, but as we brought out our wallets and produced 10-lire notes he held up his hand and asked if we couldn't make it cigarettes. I don't know what the church was going to do with cigarettes, but we gave him a couple for his trouble. In the Piazza in front of the church is the Dante Memorial.

We went to the Palazzo Vecchio in the Piazza della Signoria, built in the 13th century as a seat of the Signoria, which was a sort of Town Council, and it is still the municipal building of Florence. It contains a fine collection of paintings and sculpture. Florence is full of art galleries, the most famous being the Palazzo degli Uffizi and the Palazzo Pitti, but as all the statues and sculptures were boarded up for safety and a lot of the paintings had been removed it not was not worth trying to get round them all. In the Piazza della Signoria there are a number of statues by Bellini which were also protected by sandbags and boards.

There are six bridges over the Arno in Florence, but all except one had been blown up by the Germans as they retreated. The only remaining bridge was the Ponte Vecchio, which itself is one of the famous sights of Florence. It is lined with jewellers' shops, so that it looks like an ordinary street rather than a bridge, except for an open space in the centre where there is a small bust of Bellini. Here a long time ago Galileo watched the stars and dreamed of a telescope to help study them.

Our leave was all too brief, and it was nearly over before we realised that it was time we had some photographs taken and bought some presents to send home. It was with deep regret that we eventually had to relinquish this life of spring beds, entertainments, and general comfort, and return to our unit.

However, life could have been a great deal worse than it was at San Piero, living as we were in a good billet with little work to do. We still dined once a week with the family, and it was a pleasant change from army rations to have a meal of menestra, macaroni, polenda and wine. Every night, before going to bed, the "signora" gave us a very welcome cup of hot milk. But all good things must come to an end, and the family were every bit as sorry as we were when the time came for us to leave San Piero. The night before our departure we had a last dinner, followed by much drinking and a rousing sing-song. At 8 o'clock on the morning of Feb. 10th we pulled out.

We travelled along the familiar road through Borgo San Lorenzo to Dicomano, and then turned left into the mountains. We climbed all the way through San Godenzo and San Benedetto, then down again to the village of Rocca San Casciano. The mountain scenery was magnificent, offering some beautiful views of snow-covered peaks bathed in sunlight. Between Castrocaro and Terra del Sole we stopped for a brew-up, and about mid-day we reached our destination in Forli. We discovered that we were not due to start work until Feb 12th, so we had a day and a half in which to see the town and enjoy ourselves.

On the 12th the new D.M.A. opened, and for the next two months there was plenty of hard work. Life on the whole was nevertheless fairly pleasant, for there was no enemy action to contend with and we had regular working hours, so that all our evenings were free except when guards, etc., interfered. The whole company was quartered in what had been a huge factory. There was a big yard where we had our ration stacks, and a shed for the sacked commodities and "valuable" items such as cigarettes, chocolate, candles, and hospital supplies. There was another yard for the lorries and long sheds for the workshops, and our billets were in a building which had presumably been the factory offices.

Forli was a fairly big town, with a cinema and a theatre and a big NAAFI Canteen, the "Dorchester", similar to the Robertson Club in Florence. I had the opportunity to see another two operas, "Barber of Seville" and "Rigoletto", played by a travelling opera company. The standard of the performance was not as high as that in Florence, but nevertheless it was very good (about equal to the standard of the Carl Rosa Company in Britain) and made an excellent evening's entertainment. One really grand show I saw was the Anglo-Polish Ballet, the first ballet I had ever seen, and I thoroughly enjoyed it. Another exceptionally good show of a different type was given by the band of the D.A.F. (Desert Air Force).

The highlight of our entertainment programme while we were in Forli was that we were able to organise four platoon dances, and each one of them was a great success. We hired a small hall, a five-piece band, and by contacting people personally we were able to get ample signorinas to attend. Most of them did bring their mothers, fathers, young sisters, etc., with them, but that only served to make the evening more jolly. Sandwiches and wine were laid on, and from 7 p.m. till midnight there wasn't a boring moment. The company attempted to run a dance, but it was a complete flop. Since his return from the Jeep Platoon, the incomparable Capt. Beer had been appointed Welfare Officer, but like everything else he did he seemed to be bungling that as well. He caused a storm of indignation amongst the ranks when he issued a notice to the effect that "as it was not practicable for the entire company to attend the dance, only a limited number of tickets would be issued. Platoon sergeants are advised not to issue tickets to men whose behaviour is known to deteriorate under the influence of strong drink"! Capt. Beer was unfortunately not aware that British troops, however humble their rank may be, do not like to be treated as children. The dance was boycotted by the majority of the company, and in any case only about eight signorinas turned up.

There was one rather hectic day in Forli when the Irish Brigade celebrated St. Patrick's Day. The celebrations began with a crazy football match and ended with a crowd of crazy Irishmen firing 2 inch Mortars in the Piazza and trying to knock off the statue of a national hero from its pedestal at the top of a 100-foot column! Another party invaded the billiard room at the Dorchester and proceeded to cut bits of the green baize on the billiard tables in order to make shamrock badges for their tunic sleeves.

From February till the middle of March the whole Division was concentrated in the area around Forli, Forlimpopoli and

Russi. The infantry were doing intensive training with tanks, and it was obvious that sooner or later the big push would be launched to clear the Lombardi plains as far as the River Po. The R.A.S.C. Coys were steadily at work bringing up ammunition, and gradually the main road from Russi to the front line became bordered on either side with endless stacks of ammunition boxes. On 12th March the Division relieved 56 Div in its positions on the River Senio. Here the Germans occupied the north slope of the floodbank while we occupied the south. The Senio is not a wide river, in fact it is little more than a ditch, so that the enemy positions were only a few yards from our own. Stories came in from the infantry of teller-mines and strings of grenades being slung from one side of the river to the other whenever a German position became known, or of barrels of dynamite being rolled down the bank to explode on the other side.

This situation lasted for just under a month, until finally on April 9th the first blow was struck on the last colossal offensive.

THE FINAL OFFENSIVE

All afternoon we gazed up at the sky as hundreds of planes passed overhead to drop 170,000 fragmentation bombs on Jerrie's forward positions. In the evening the windows of our billets rattled and shook and the horizon was a shimmering mass of gunflashes as a terrific artillery barrage was "laid down". At 19.20 hours the 2nd New Zealand and 8th Indian Divisions of 5th Corps attacked across the Senio and made swift progress in spite of bitterly fighting German rearguards. On the left flank of the 8th Army front the 3rd Carpathian Division of the Polish Corps forged slowly ahead up Highway 9 towards Bologna, while on the extreme right the Cremona Italian Combat Group advanced towards Argenta. This was the situation as explained to us by Capt. Fowell on the first day of the offensive. 78 Div did not take part in the attack that breached the Senio line; their role was to be one of exploitation until bridgeheads had been won over the next river, the Santerno. On April 10th the Division poured across the Senio into the Concentration Areas around Lugo. On the night of the 11th the Santerno was crossed and 78 Div passed through into the bridgehead established by Indian and New Zealand troops. Then with 36 Brigade on the left, 38 Brigade on the right, and supported by 2nd Armoured Brigade, the infantry turned north and cleared all the ground between the Santerno and the Sillaro up to Bastia on the River Reno.

By this time, 722 D.M.A. had come to an end, and on April 14th, after a big carousal on the previous night, we pulled out of Forli. We travelled only about 20 miles through Russi to Lugo, where we camped for the night. It was a tribute to the welfare services that in the recently liberated town we were able to drop in at a canteen and go to a cinema show that same evening. On the morning of the 15th we struck camp and moved off again through the heavily bombed areas near the Santerno River, such as the completely razed village of San Lorenzo, to a point near the village of Santa Maria, in the flat, open country. Here we pitched our tents again under some trees and set up 726 D.M.A. We were only here for a few days, during which vast quantities of ammunition, petrol and rations were received from the rear areas and issued to the divisional units with none of the careful checking and accounting which was the rule in more static times. One night two German planes came over, the last we were to see of the Luftwaffe, and did a bit of strafing all round us.

The Germans, having withdrawn from their previous river lines, were trying to make a stand on the Reno, fighting for time to man the defences of the Argenta gap, a neck of land between vast flooded areas which we must pass through in order to reach the vital Po bridges. The gap was bounded on the east by Lake Commachio and the marshes that fringed it and on the west by the Reno and its swamps. A series of devastating blows were delivered at the Argenta line, all nine infantry battalions being engaged. The 2nd Lancashire Fusiliers made the first bridge over the tank-proof Fossa Marina canal, and the 2nd Inniskillings finally cut off Argenta from the north. 36 Brigade then pushed through and broke out of this great defensive belt of minefields and cleverly sited weapons, and the Germans started a confused withdrawal.

On the 21st we closed 726 D.M.A. and moved off again along dust-ridden roads through Argenta, arriving at a new location in the open country north of the town. These were hectic days, and the situation changed so rapidly that it was never possible to foresee when the next move would take place or where it would take us to. Our troops had met more strong resistance along the line of the Fossa di Porto, but after a hard fight the canal was crossed and on the 22nd the Po di Volano was reached, the last river before the Po itself.

On the 23rd we were away again, still going north through Portomaggiore to another camping-ground near the village of Voghiero. All this time our daily routine consisted of one morning parade, a few hours work and the rest of the day free. The infantry had quickly crossed the Po di Volano, and the

Germans vainly tried to get their troops back behind the Po. Remnants of the 76 Panzer Corps struggled to defend the last pontoons over the Po, but by 25th April the whole Eighth Army was up to the river. All resistance was smashed, and 78 Division was then concentrated around Ferrara, while the rest of 5 Corps went on to Venice and Trieste. Thus, three weeks after the offensive began, we were encamped in an area that was strewn with enemy tanks, guns and transport, and thousands upon thousands of prisoners. It was a wonderful sight, a sight to which we had looked forward throughout many a long, hellish winter, when victory had seemed hopelessly remote, sometimes almost impossible. Even now I think few of us realised how near this was to the end, not of a phase in the war, but of the whole odious epoch.

On the 26th April we had a day pass in Ferrara, only two days after the Germans had been chased out. The civilians were still fighting a fire in one of the big buildings in the centre of the town. There is a fine cathedral in Ferrara, and although the external architecture is not as impressive as the Duomo in Florence the interior is one of the most beautiful I've ever seen. In front of the huge altar we saw the coffins, draped with Italian flags and many wreaths, of 7 partisans who had been captured by the Germans and then shot before the Nazis left the town. There was also a wreath placed on the spot where they had been murdered. There was little else of interest in the town, but the welfare services had lost no time, and there were two canteens, an ENSA show, and three cinemas available. The Teatro Nuovo, where the ENSA show was held, is one of the best theatres I've been in in Italy, elaborately decorated and very comfortable. In the evening the kilted pipe bands of the 1st & 8th A. & S.H. played in the cathedral square and drew great crowds.

On the 28th a movement order came in, and about 2 p.m. we pushed off. First of all we went over several miles of rough tracks to C.R.A.S.C., then carried on in a thunderstorm and torrential rain to Ferrara, where we joined the convoy of the Div. advance party, heading north. The roads after Ferrara were pretty good, and it wasn't long before we reached the River Po. We crossed the river by means of a masterpiece among bridges, a sort of Bailey Bridge on barges, similar to a pontoon bridge but much more highly developed. The river is very wide, and the bridge was obviously a praise-worthy feat of rapid engineering. Having reached the other side, we turned right and travelled eastwards along the north bank for about 10 miles until we reached a small town. Here we went off the main road and followed a third class road for a few more miles to another small town called Crespino. The civilians in this area all turned out to wave at us, as we were amongst the first British troops they had seen, and they all seemed very happy about it. A surprising thing was that the German defences along the banks of the river were very poor. All one could see was a long line of trenches and a few dug-outs, but no pill boxes or concrete turrets such as we had seen further south. There were not many derelict vehicles by the side of the road, nearly all the German Army having been trapped north of the Po, but quite a number of horses were roaming about the fields.

At Crespino we moved into a factory of some sort which made a very good billet, and the local people were so amiable that it seemed as if we were going to have a very nice time here. On the following morning, however, while we were getting things ready to receive the expected load of rations for the new D.M.A., the order came in for us to pack up and go back where we came from. The usual confusion. So with many regrets we moved off again, and were crossing the Po once more about mid-day, this time a bit further up the river at Occhiobello. This bridge was a regular wooden pontoon bridge on collapsible floats. We were soon back in Ferrara again, and then succeeded in taking the wrong road out of the town, so that we were nearly back in Argenta again before the leader of our little convoy decided to turn back. We retraced our steps to Ferrara, got on the right road, and after about half an hour arrived at our old location, tired, hungry, and browned off.

We were still here on May 2nd, when at 9 p.m. we heard the special announcement that hostilities in Italy had ceased and that all German forces in North Italy and the remaining parts of Austria had been surrendered to General Alexander at Caserta. Celebrations were commenced immediately, and it wasn't long before everyone was joining in a general open-air moonlight spree. Two gallons of rum appeared mysteriously from under someone's bed, bottles of vino were extracted from kit-bags, V-shaped petrol fires were lit, distant fires dotted the surrounding countryside, flares rose and fell, and tracers lined the sky. The festivities went on far into the night.

On May 3rd the platoon was split into two parties, and after a great deal of loading and off-loading kits and G.1098 I set off with one party. We went a few miles down the road to take over the stocks of 131 B.I.D. and supervise the ferrying forward of the same stocks. We occupied excellent billets here, in a factory on the outskirts of bomb-shattered Portomaggiore, where we had very little work to do, and it was a pity that the job was so short-lived.

On May 5th we travelled north again and re-joined the rest of the company in a barracks at Pordenone, an excellent big town. There were hundreds of partisans walking about here, armed to the teeth with tommy-guns, rifles, grenades, etc., while we went about unarmed. The civilians referred to us as the "army without arms."

On May 9th we formed part of the long convoy which drove over the Carnic Alps by the Santa Croce Pass into Austria. 78 Division took over the occupation of the province of Carinthia, a country of mighty mountains and beautiful lakes, of great forests and swift-flowing rivers, of leather shorts and dirndl skirts, and, above all, of Viennese Waltzes.

Six months later, in November 1945, I was on my way home through Switzerland and France. I crossed the Channel and landed at Folkestone on November 22nd, exactly three years since I first set out from Woking, Surrey, on an overseas draft.

Timeline of Principal Events

1942

November 25th – Woking, Newcastle, Edinburgh, Wishaw.

November 27th – Glasgow, Paisley, Gourock. "Llangibby Castle" troopship.

November 28th – Sea Voyage begins.

December 4th – Straits of Gibraltar.

December 5th – Gibraltar. Transfer to "Llanstephan Castle".

December 6th – Leave Gibraltar.

December 8th – Algiers.

December 20th – Algiers to Birmandries.

December 22nd – Posted to "Forward Area". Back to Algiers then La Perouse.

December 23rd – March to Rouiba. Train to Souk Ahras.

December 25th – Detrain. March to Zarouria.

December 27th – Zarouria to Souk Ahras. Board train to Guelma. March to Millessimo No.1 Gen Base Depot Aerodrome.

1943

January 7th – Millessimo to Guelma. Train to Ghardimaou on Algeria-Tunisia border.

January 9th – Detrain. Drafted to 78th Division.

January 13th – Train to Souk el Arba.

January 14th – Truck to Sidi Smail. Report to 11th Infantry Brigade. Sent to 78 Division Troop Company. Sent to B Transport Platoon, 36th Infantry Brigade. 78 Division holds front line between Sedjenane and El Aroussa. "Longstop Hill" and "Banana Ridge" close by. Remain at Beja for 2 weeks. Convoys to various locations including Sidi Smail and Souk el Arba.

February 3rd – Leave Beja. Travel to Medjez el Bab. Posted to Composite Platoon (Supply Platoon).

February 20th – Germans attack. All available men sent to Medjez Station to defend it. 7 weeks at Teboursouk.

March 23rd – 78 Division pulled off line for a rest.

April 2nd – Back to line at Teboursouk.

April 18th – Leave Teboursouk. Attacked by German aircraft.

April 24th – Move to Toukabeur.

May 7th – Attack begins.

May 8th – Company moves to Medjez.

May 9th – Tunis falls. Company heads for Tunis.

May 15th – 20th Birthday.

May 30th – Depart Tunis. Head back to Millessimo in Algeria for three weeks.

June 20th – Back to Grombalia in Tunisia. Parade for Montgomery. 78 Division inducted into 8th Army.

July 26th – Embark assault landing craft at Sousse. Depart North Africa for Sicily.

July 28th – Arrive at Avola in Sicily 6 or 7 days after initial landings.

July 29th – Convoy inland to south of Centuripe.

August 3rd – Centuripe captured.

August 10th – Move through Centuripe to Adrano beside Mount Etna. Camp for two weeks.

August 28th – Move to Brolo near the coast.

September 3rd – Italy invaded.

September 25th – Arrive in Messina.

September 26th – Depart Messina and Sicily across the Straits of Messina. Land at 10.00 near San Giovanni Calabria.

September 27th – East Coast of 'The Toe' to Crotone.

September 28th – Leave Crotone heading round 'Instep' to Taranto.

September 30th – Drive north to Bari, then on to Barletta.

October – Carry on to Serracapriola. Find billet in Franciscan Monastery. Attack by 4 German tanks while supplying Argylls with Ammunition at River Trigno. Move on to Campomarino at end of October, then on to Casalbordino near River Sangro.

November 29th – Attack on Sangro begins.

Early December – 2nd Canadian Division relieve 78th Division. Camp near village of Montagno.

December 17th – Hospital. Stays for seven days.

December 24th – Returns to Platoon at Montagno.

1944

January 4th – Move out after roads cleared of snow towards Appenines. Remain at Pescolanciano for several weeks.

February 5th – 78th Division moves to village of Agnone.

February 18th – Most of Platoon moves out, Fergus and others have to remain to escort Poles to supply dumps. Snow makes roads impassable and they have to remain with Poles for two weeks.

March 4th – Move out to find rest of company near village of Ponte Latone.

March 15th – Pull out onto Route 6, the road to Cassino.

March 18th – Platoon mustered and ordered to Mignano in preparation for attack over Rapido River at Cassino. Remain here one week. Constant shelling. Strafed by enemy Stukas.

March 24th – Back to previous location as River attack doesn't happen.

April 10th – Dangerous supply duty at Cassino. Under heavy mortar fire.

April 12th – 72 hours leave granted. First since leaving England.

April 14th – Visit Pompeii.

April 15th – Visit Sorrento.

April 16th – Depart Mairoi to Route 6 and Company location.

April 17th – Detail to Presengaro. Posted to 57th Infantry Brigade Coy.

April 19th – Taken to Composite Platoon based north of Capua.

April 30th – Struck down by Malaria. Transferred to hospital at Cancello.

May 4th – Hospital train overnight to Barletta then Bari General hospital. 10 days in hospital.

May 15th – 21st Birthday.

May 17th – Depart for 159 transit camp near Naples while helping to guard 8 German prisoners. 5 escape at Foggia.

May 18th – Visit to Naples.

May 20th – Move to camp at Nola, 15 miles from Naples.

May 28th – Depart Nola to Vairano. Sees 2 Spitfires crash.

June 4th – Move from Vairano on Route 6 north past Cassino.

June 9th – Pass through outskirts of Rome. Continue north on Route 3.

June 15th – North through Ronciglione to Viterbo.

June 17th – North through Orvieto to San Lorenzo.

June 23rd – Shelled all night. Germans still holding out at Castaglione del Lago.

June 24th – Large attack dislodges Germans.

June 27th – Set up supply dump on plains.

July 5th – 78 Division informed they were coming out of line and being sent to Egypt. First big proper break in two years of constant duty. Camp at Tivoli.

July 6th – Day pass into Rome.

July 7th – South on Route 6, then inland to Benevento.

July 8th – Through Foggia to Bari.

July 9th – Arrive in Taranto. Spend a week here.

July 18th – Depart Taranto for Mediterranean and Egypt.

July 23rd – Disembark at Port Said. Board train to Quassasin. Trucks to camp.

July 26th – 5 days leave in Cairo.

July 31st – Return to Quassasin.

September 7th – Train to Port Said. 3 days on "Capetown Castle".

September 10th – Depart Port Said.

September 15th – Arrive in Taranto.

September 26th – Move north to Gillianova.

October 1st – Visit Senegallia for the day.

October 2nd – Move out towards the front line again. Nightmare journey overnight to reach Assisi.

October 4th – Through Borgo San Lorenzo to Scarperia. Spend 4 weeks here. Monte Grande battleground 20 miles away.

November 14th – Move to Firenzuola. 3 weeks here.

December 9th – Sent with squad to Castel del Rio, 15 miles from Firenzuola.

December 25th – Christmas in Castel del Rio.

December 28th – Move to San Piero. Billeted with local family.

1945

January 2nd – Seconded to Jeep Platoon on forward area. 3 weeks delivering ammunition etc.

January 26th – Jeep Platoon duty over. Returns to 57 Coy at San Piero.

January 28th – 7 days leave in Florence.

February 4th – Back to San Piero.

February 10th – Pull out of San Piero to Forli. 2 months in Forli.

April 14th – Move out of Forli. To Lugo.

April 15th – Move out to Santa Maria.

April 21st – Move off through Argenta.

April 23rd – Head north to Voghiero.

April 28th – Move out of camp heading north. Cross River Po. On to town of Crespino.

May 2nd – Announcement of German surrender in Italy.

May 3rd – Sent to supply dump at Portomaggiore.

May 5th – North to Pordenone.

May 9th – Drive over Alps by Santa Croce Pass into Austria.

Spends 6 months in Province of Carinthia.

November 1945 – Returns through Switzerland and France.

November 22nd – Back in England exactly 3 years after leaving.